How to Prophetically Pray on Purpose

By

Dr. Robert L. Bailey, Jr.

Copyright © 2020 by Dr. Robert L. Bailey, Jr.
Printed in the United States of America

ISBN: 978-0-578-65305-1 (paperback)

All rights reserved. No part of this publication may be reproduced, stored in a retrieval system, or transmitted in any form or by any means electronic, mechanical, photocopying, recording or otherwise-without the prior permission of the publisher.

www.restorationofpraise.org

Table of Contents

Foreword by Bishop Larry Donnell Leonard, Sr.   vii
Foreword by Pastor Christopher F. Hartwell   x
Foreword by Pastor J. Moss   xi
The Introduction   xiii

1. Understanding How to Pray   1
2. What Does it Mean to Prophetically Pray   7
3. What Happens When Prayer Meets Praise   11
4. How to Identify Your Purpose in God's Plan   17
5. How to Stop The Enemy From Stopping Your Prayers   23
6. Watch What You Release and How You Release It   32
7. "The (A) Prayer of Power"   35
8. "The (B) Prayer of Power"   37
9. "The (C) Prayer of Power"   39
10. "The (D) Prayer of Power"   41
11. "The (E) Prayer of Power"   43
12. "The (F) Prayer of Power"   45
13. "The (G) Prayer of Power"   47
14. "The (H) Prayer of Power"   49
15. "The (I) Prayer of Power"   51
16. "The (J) Prayer of Power"   53
17. "The (K) Prayer of Power"   55
18. "The (L) Prayer of Power"   57
19. "The (M) Prayer of Power"   59

20. "The (N) Prayer of Power"	61
21. "The (O) Prayer of Power"	63
22. "The (P) Prayer of Power"	65
23. "The (Q) Prayer of Power"	67
24. "The (R) Prayer of Power"	69
25. "The (S) Prayer of Power"	71
26. "The (T) Prayer of Power"	73
27. "The (U) Prayer of Power"	75
28. "The (V) Prayer of Power"	77
29. "The (W) Prayer of Power"	79
30. "The (X) Prayer of Power"	81
31. "The (Y) Prayer of Power"	82
32. "The (Z) Prayer of Power"	83
"The (A To Z) Prayer of Power"	85
The Outroduction	87
The Gift For Your Support	91
About The Author	93

This Book is dedicated to

The Bailey Family, Zahra' Bailey (Wife);
Zaila Rainn Bailey (Daughter);
Mary Bailey (Grandmother); Shirley Bailey (Mom); Toni Ned (Sister); Roshun Bailey-Constant (Sister); Benjamin Bailey (Brother) And In Loving Memory of Rev. Robert L. Bailey, Sr. & Deacon Robert T. Upshaw
Recognizing The Entire Upshaw Family

Every since I have met Pastor Bailey (Robert), I found him to be extremely excited about preaching, teaching and living the word of God. It is very much seen in his choice of words and the passion by which he exposes with intimate fashion the Word to every listener and reader.

You will discover exactly what I mean once you read the first few words of this special presentation. It will be obvious that he does not only share the word with passion and intentionality but he has spent quality and quantity time in the presence of our Father. Be aware in the most positive way that he takes a praise break throughout this potent piece of work.

Those who read this work are not just opening another book on prayer but are led into the glorious presence of Jehovah with some powerful and meaningful examples. The examples are not so practical that they are not spiritual. They have been bathed in prayer and praise. Robert has taken an interesting approach to declaring and decreeing, binding and loosing with the twin powers of prayer and praise. The beauty of the scriptures used lends themselves to the documentation of points made thus yielding to revelatory inspiration.

Thank you Robert for your transparency, vulnerability, and boldness to place before us a part of your own personal ecclesiastical body of work and experience. Thank you for hearing and obeying the Spirit of God for such a time as this. Now let us prophetically pray after we have read and embraced this important piece of work.

Bishop Larry Donnell Leonard, Sr.

Have you ever felt like God put you in timeout? Have you ever felt like God was playing hide and seek? It is the frustration of the unanswered questions. Sometimes we make prayer too difficult. Lord, do I not believe enough? Instead of beginning with prayer, we often resort to it after all other resources have been used. When we come to the end of ourselves, we come to the beginning with God.

Prayer is the most powerful but unused agent in the Believers arsenal. In fact, prayer is becoming an endangered species in the Kingdom of God. The abuse, misuse, and disuse of prayers are threatening this necessary agent into extinction. Prayer is the central avenue God uses to transform our hearts. People who don't want peaceful progress don't pray. We have been taught that everything in the universe has been set, so why pray? God is not going to change His mind. How can a finite being enter into a dialogue with an infinite Creator? There are over 3500 promises in the Bible. Some believers are reluctant to believe a promise for fear that they will be disappointed by God, so they live with no expectation and they pray for less to keep from being frustrated or let down.

Pastor Bailey provides the reader with a description and definition of prophetic prayers. He shows us that prophetic praying is not only an action, but an attitude as well. Your thinking creates your reality. Beliefs are things we accept as true based on repeated thoughts and messages we receive and the behaviors we witness. Sometimes beliefs are based on the perception of reality. Your distorted beliefs could be holding you back.

Pastor Bailey provides the reader with alphabetized affirmations through alliteration. This book on prophetic praying is designed for one to experience the power and presence of God. This book also intends to assist us in maintaining our purpose and passion for prophetic praying. Enjoy your journey of illumination as you read this manual on prophetic praying.

— Pastor Christopher F. Hartwell
Crossroads Community Church, Houston, TX
(Pastor Bailey's Pastor)

When I was elevated to the Pastorate, the Lord revealed to me that Christianity through complex and often misinterpreted doctrine, had become cumbersome and hopelessly out of reach for the non-believer and those that had fallen. God's instruction to me was to "Make It Plain ... Simplify my precepts for my people and show them that I am yet just a PRAYER away. After indulging in this reading by Pastor Dr. Robert Bailey, Jr., it really hit home for me and my assignment as a Pastor.

"How to Prophetically Pray on Purpose" takes an often intimidating and overwhelming subject such as Prayer and The Prophetic relationship between the two and walks the reader through it so that readers of all ages and seasons will profit from it. Showing us not only HOW to pray and pray prophetically, but also showing us what to do before, during and after we pray.

This is a must-read and a great tool for ministries to use as a guide when presenting the subject of Prayer to the people of God. This is a definite "Go-To" reference in the journey of my assignment.

— Pastor J. Moss
Living Waters Church, Detroit, MI
(PraiseDome Detroit)

The Introduction

As you read this book, you will uncover divine information and prayers of prophetic utterance that can be of spiritual importance. These are simple yet relevant prayers of power that may be used to enhance your prayer time and help position you in God's plan for your life. You will find each prayer as an alphabetical declaration which has a direct and divine promise that's combined and cosigned with PRAISE. These PRAYERS are designed to PRODUCE power, strength, peace, and joy, along with other spiritual virtues and characteristics of the Holy Spirit. **Galatians 5:22, 23 (KJV)**, *"But the fruit of the Spirit is love, joy, peace, longsuffering, gentleness, goodness, faith, meekness, temperance: against such there is no law."* I'm a firm believer that PRAYER + PRAISE = PRODUCTION. In other words, when your FAITH lines up with God's FAVOR, it will be FRUITFUL for your life. Through these Prophetic prayers, you are destined to unlock God's power and unveil promises every time you read them prophetically over your life, even into the lives of others.

Each prayer is proven to provoke God to prove His work in, over, and around your life. The Bible declares in **Malachi 3:10 (KJV)**, *"Bring ye all the tithes* **(time, talents, treasure, and thanksgiving)** *into the storehouse* **(the place of sowing)**, *that there may be meat* **(supply; supplies to function)** *in mine house, and prove* **(try; to establish authenticity)** *me now herewith* **(right here, right now, with whatever you need or desire)**, *saith the Lord of hosts, if I will not open you the windows of heaven, and pour you out a* **(singular)** *blessing, that there shall not be room enough* **(unlimited amount)** *to receive it."* Basically, God says for us to bring all that we have and are to Him in our requests, establish authenticity in His authority, try Him RIGHT HERE,

Robert L. Bailey

RIGHT NOW, WITH WHATEVER YOU NEED AND/OR DESIRE. As you do this, watch the windows of Heaven abundantly pour out the very blessing you need. So, as you read this book, read it prophetically to declare the power of God's Word, work, worth, and wealth in your life. Sit back, relax and be bountifully blessed as you learn, "HOW TO PROPHETICALLY PRAY ON PURPOSE!"

Understanding How to Pray

Luke 18:1 (NIV) - *"Then Jesus told his disciples a parable to show them that they should ALWAYS PRAY and not give up."*

Let's start with the basics. What is PRAYER? Prayer is a personal yet spiritual communion and communication with God; a devout petition or request to God made in worship, adoration, and/or thanksgiving. When we pray, there is a divine and direct connection to the Father through His Son, Jesus Christ under the unction of the Holy Spirit, which taps into the production and prosperity of His power. The bible says in **James 5:15, 16 (KJV)**, *"And the prayer of faith shall save the sick, and the Lord shall raise him up; and if he have committed sins, they shall be forgiven him. Confess your faults one to another, and pray one for another, that ye may be healed. The effectual fervent prayer of a righteous man availeth much."* In other words, your PRAYER OF FAITH will produce a PLACE OF FRUITFULNESS that commands and demands a move of the Most High God in your life.

When and after you pray, you must be confident that what you've prayed for will come to pass. Prayer, just like faith, is worthless if you don't believe the results will work out in your favor. **Isaiah 43:10 (KJV)**, *"Ye are my witnesses, saith the Lord, and my servant whom I have chosen: that ye may know and believe me, and understand that I am he: before me there was no God formed, neither shall there be after me."* When you seal your prayer with praise, you basically become a witness to the work of the Lord and you operate in the belief that GOD IS THE ONLY ANSWER you need. THERE IS NOTHING or NOBODY GREATER!!

Jesus, in His instructions to man, gave us a specific prayer to be used as a model. He said in **Matthew 6:9-13 (KJV)**, *"After this manner therefore pray ye: Our Father which art in heaven, Hallowed be thy name. Thy kingdom come, Thy will be done on earth, as it is in heaven. Give us this day our daily bread. And forgive us our debts, as we forgive our debtors. And lead us not into temptation, but deliver us from evil: For thine is the kingdom, and the power, and the glory, forever. Amen."* This model was given to the people to teach them how to incorporate prayer into their lives. This outline is a basis of prayer, however as you grow in God, your prayer method should turn into a prayer formula. What is the PRAYER FORMULA? The prayer formula is called A.C.T.S. which literally means that after you A.C.T., God automatically ACTS! Here's the A.C.T.S. Formula:

(A) Acknowledge God

In praying, we should ACKNOWLEDGE God for WHO HE IS because of our personal salvation and testimony of what He's done in our lives. We have to remember WHO we're addressing. God (Hebrew: Abba "The Father") is a sovereign God.

"Isaiah 48:17 (KJV), *"Thus saith the Lord, thy Redeemer, the Holy One of Israel; I am the Lord thy God which teacheth thee to profit, which leadeth thee by the way that thou shouldest go."* This means prosperity will come into my life only through the acknowledgment of God the Father. Remember, He is

OMNIPOTENT (all-powerful)
OMNISCIENT (all-knowing)
OMNI-PRESENT (everywhere; always present)
OMNIFICENT (unlimited power of creation)
OMNI-DIRECTIONAL (moves in all directions)

The bible says in **Proverbs 3:5, 6 (KJV)**, *"Trust in the Lord with all thine heart; and lean not unto thine own understanding. In all thy ways acknowledge him, and he shall direct thy paths."* Thus, we should always

ACKNOWLEDGE Him first in our prayers to ensure the best result towards the promise. Here's an example:

> "Father in the name of Jesus, I bless your Holy and righteous name. I magnify you, give you Glory, honor and praise you for who you are. Not just for what you've done, but mainly for who you are to me. For you are awesome, magnificent, glorious, mighty, marvelous, wonderful, you reign supreme and there is none like or greater than you."

(C) Confess To God

In praying, we should be ready to submit any sins we may have committed that would hinder the production of the promise from coming to pass. The confession of our sins, mistakes, shortcomings, and faults are made to God and not to man. For David declared in **Psalms 51:3, 4 (KJV)**, *"For I acknowledge my transgressions: and my sin is ever before me. Against thee* **(God)**, *thee only, have I sinned, and done this evil in thy sight: that thou mightest be justified when thou speakest, and be clear when thou judgest."* That is to say, we should seek God for divine restoration and forgiveness when we have sinned and come short of His Glory. The Bible states in **Romans 3:23 (KJV)**, *"For ALL have sinned, and come short of the glory of God."* This leads me to believe that no one is exempt from sin. Remember, there are sins we commit that we have knowledge of and those we have no knowledge. It's vitally important to always seek forgiveness in ALL things known and unknown. Please understand that every sin is wrapped up into one of three categories according to **1 John 2:16 (KJV)**, *"For all that is in the world, (1) the lust of the flesh, and (2) the lust of the eyes, and (3) the pride of life, is not of the Father, but is of the world."*

WARNING Forget everything you were ever told in the statement,

"What you don't know won't hurt you." That statement is a lie. What you DO NOT know CAN AND WILL HURT YOU, especially when it deals with sin. The Bible says in **Proverbs 28:13 (KJV)**, *"He that covereth his sins shall not prosper: but whoso confesseth and forsaketh them shall have mercy."* It also says in **1 John 1:8, 9 (KJV)**, *"If we say that we have no sin, we deceive ourselves, and the truth is not in us. If we confess our sins, He* **(God)** *is faithful and just to forgive us our sins, and to cleanse us from ALL unrighteousness."* Simply put, confession is good for your soul. Here's an example:

> "Father, please forgive me for any and everything I've done knowing and unknowing. I have sinned and come short of your Glory, but seek your forgiveness. Have mercy on me and cover me with the blood of your precious son, that cleanses me from all unrighteousness. Shield and protect my soul from all mistakes, mess-ups, faults, failures, hurts and pains as I purify my life in your presence, power and provision. I want to be productive to you and the Kingdom."

(T) Thank God

When we pray, we should never forget to THANK GOD. As a matter of fact, we should thank God for everything. We provoke the Spirit of increase and abundance when we thank Him. He becomes more inclined to manifest the promises in our lives. In **Ephesians 3:20 (KJV)** the Bible declares, *"Now unto him that is able to do exceeding abundantly above all that we ask or think, according to the power that worketh in us."* Basically, it's in the power we possess that provokes the promise of more. As children of God praising Him is what we were created to do and when we showcase a THANKFUL ATTITUDE, it produces a TRIUMPHANT ALTITUDE.

"Psalms 100:1, 2, 4 (KJV), *"Make a joyful noise unto the Lord, all ye* lands. *Serve the Lord with gladness: come before his presence with singing."* It then goes on to say, *"Enter into his gates with thanksgiving, and into his courts with praise: be thankful unto him, and bless his name."* So, when we THINK about Him or what He's doing or has done in our lives, there should be a THANKFUL response done joyfully and loudly with excitement and enthusiasm. I believe right here is a great place to stick that THANKFUL PRAISE. Glory! Hallelujah! Here's an example:

> "Lord God, I thank you for all you've done, all you're doing, and all you're about to do in my life. I bless you for the highs and lows, the ups and downs, the good and bad, because I realize it's all working together for my good. I even thank you for holding back the hand, hindrances, and hurts of the enemy while keeping me and everything connected to me safe from harm and danger. Lord God, I thank you."

(S) Seal It With His Signature

We need to remember to seal every prayer in the name of Jesus. Why? Because Jesus is the mediator between us and God and He assures that every prayer request is heard and the promises will come to pass. The Bible says in **John 14:6 (KJV)**, *"Jesus saith unto him, I am the way, the truth, and the life: no man cometh unto the Father, but by me."* In essence, to get direction, clarity, understanding, power, strength, miracles and/or spiritual manifestations from God, you must go through His Son. Jesus seals the production of the promise.

Understand that the name **JESUS** means *"Jehovah Saves Us."* This is why we identify Him as Savior. He's the One who saves us from the condemnation of sin and the wrath of God. Because of this, we should end our prayers with the SEAL OF THE SAVIOR! **Romans 10:13 (KJV)** says, *"For whosoever shall call upon the name of the Lord shall be saved."* When we call on the name of the Lord, He automatically moves to rescue us from whatever, whomever and wherever we may find ourselves. The psalmist says in **Psalms 148:13 (KJV)**, *"Let them praise the name of the Lord: for his name alone is excellent; his glory is above the earth and heaven."* **Isaiah 9:6 (KJV)** also declares, *"For unto us a child is born, unto us a son is given: and the government shall be upon his shoulder: and His name shall be called Wonderful, Counselor, The Mighty God, The everlasting Father, The Prince of Peace."* Essentially, it's important to seal our prayers and praise with "IN THE NAME OF JESUS CHRIST OUR LORD" or "IN JESUS NAME" which is the Signature of the Savior.

During this time, you are also released to cancel the schemes of Satan. Scripture teaches us in **Matthew 18:18 (KJV)**, *"Verily I say unto you, Whatsoever ye shall bind on earth shall be bound in heaven: and whatsoever ye shall loose on earth shall be loose in heaven."* In this, God has given you the divine authority to bind the devil and his evil plans as well as loose the Holy Spirit and the angelic authorities to assist you. Here's an example:

> "Father, in the name of Jesus I cancel every assignment, attachment, activity, act, and attack of the enemy sent to destroy, disturb, or distract my walk with you and I command the release of your Divine favor and order to be fruitful in my life. Dispatch Angels to minister in every area and meet every need, fulfill every promise, and manifest yourself mightily in my life. I seal this prayer with expectancy and excitement, AND IT IS SO in the mighty, marvelous and majestic name of Jesus, I shout and celebrate. AMEN!"

If you're reading this book and don't know how to pray or what to say when you pray, you can follow this productive formula to establish, develop, and continue a productive prayer life.

What Does it Mean to Prophetically Pray

Praying is something that anyone and/or everyone can do. Even though we've been given a method for praying, prayer is simply your personal communication with God. Prayer is not something that you do to impress others with creative words or a melodic intonation, but it's the spirit in which the prayer is uttered that will cause a shift in the Spirit realm.

Matthew 6:5, 7 (KJV), *"And when thou prayest, thou shalt not be as the hypocrites are: for they love to pray standing in the synagogues and in the corners of the streets, that they may be seen of men. Verily I say unto you, They have their reward. But when ye pray, use not vain repetitions as the heathen do: for they think that they shall be heard for their much speaking."* It's not about what you say when you pray, but it's the attitude of your spirit when you're requesting and/or pulling on the heart of God. Whether you know this or not, you've been given Divine keys to unlock and unleash the divine manifestation you need in your life through Prophetic prayers. **Proverbs 18:21 (KJV)** reads, *"Death and life are in the power of the tongue* **(your utterance)**: *and they that love it shall eat the fruit thereof."* You have authority and your words have weight and worth. When you pray, be careful not to release something prophetically unaware because you can and will eat it.

Many of us have been taught how to pray. However, there is a different release in Prophetic praying. What is Prophetic praying and what will it do, you ask?"Well, Prophetic prayers are prayers spoken with Divine inspiration and devoted expectation. When we prophetically pray, we open up the SUPERNATURAL provision of God. To put the matter another way, in Prophetic praying, we provoke God's SUPER on the NATURAL in our lives. Thus, through these strategic prayers, God is moved to manifest miracles, signs and wonders and He makes sure that every request is rewarded openly. In **Hebrews 2:4 (KJV)** the Bible reads, *"God also bearing them witness, both with signs and wonders, and with divers miracles, and gifts of the Holy Ghost, according to his own will."* Prophetic praying brings your purpose into perspective. Please understand that purpose is your intent to reach your destiny. You can't change your destiny because destiny is already determined. However, at any time during your life, you can alter your purpose but it's through prophetic praying that will redirect you back towards your destiny.

Prophetic praying also means to declare or foresee a certain outcome INTO existence. This type of prayer life changes the dynamics of basic praying (FOR the existence of something; ex. "Thy kingdom come, thy will be done... etc.") into prophetically praying (declaring that something INTO existence; ex. "I declare your kingdom to come NOW, and that your WILL IS ALREADY done in my life and those surrounding me). When you decree in Prophetic prayer, it's to invoke the movement of major manifestations in our lives through declaration and not just through petition. For the bible says in **Psalms 73:28 (KJV)**, *"But it is good for me to draw near to God: I have put my trust in the Lord God, that I may declare all thy works."* Expressly, PROPHETIC DECLARATION brings DIVINE REVELATION into OPEN MANIFESTATION. Now that's something to shout about!

This kind of prayer is done in the Spirit, with spiritual and physical results. It's through this type of prayer life that clarity and understanding of spiritual maneuvering is made manifest.

"1 Corinthians 14:15 (KJV), *"What is it then? I will pray with the spirit, and I will pray with the understanding also: I will sing with the spirit, and I will sing with the understanding also."* When we pray in the Spirit, then the Spirit of the Lord bears witness to it and brings that very thing into existence. That's why Solomon said in **Proverbs 16:3 (KJV)**, *"Commit thy works unto the Lord, and thy thoughts shall be established."* Let me simplify this for you. God promises to take your WORKS along with His WORD and WISDOM then make something WONDERFUL out of it. That's why we sing and shout that "God is a WONDER because He performs WONDROUS acts, which make Him WONDERFUL." Let me pause for a praise break. Glory! Thank you Lord God for being wonderful to me!

So why is prophetic praying so important? Well I'm glad you asked. Prophetic prayers are important because it gives you the power to speak boldly of the things you expect God to bring to pass according to His Word. This kind of praying shakes the ground of what you expect God to grant you! It's our Prophetic prayers that open up REVELATION, RELEASE, and REWARD. Jesus gives us an example in **Luke 3:21, 22 (KJV)**, *"Now when all the people were baptized, it came to pass, that Jesus also being baptized, and PRAYING, the heaven was opened* **(revelation)**. *And the Holy Ghost descended in a bodily shape like a dove upon him* **(release)**, *and a voice came from heaven, which said, Thou art my beloved Son; in thee I am well pleased* **(reward)**." Because of this prayer I've come to the conclusion that this was Prophetic. Heaven opened immediately after the prayer which signified a Divine move of God. In this we see what revelation is; God's total disclosure of Himself and His will to those who desire it. So when Jesus prays, REVELATION comes by God opening up the Heaven, then RELEASE takes place when the Holy Spirit rests on the requester, and then REWARD is given when God says that, "He was well pleased."

Maybe this scripture will help also. Luke, the physician said in **Luke 22:41-43 (KJV)**, *"And he was withdrawn from them about a stone's cast, and kneeled down, and prayed, Saying, Father, if thou be willing, remove this cup from me: nevertheless not my will, but thine, be done* **(meaning, God give me the strength)**. *And there appeared an angel unto him from heaven,* *strengthening him* **(meaning, strength was given)**." This passage leads us to believe that when Jesus prays in this text, it must have been Prophetic because of what happens afterwards. The text mentioned is tailored to teach us that when Jesus prayed, God dispatched angels to give Him what He asked for. We must believe that if and when we do the same thing Jesus did, it will produce the same results. The REWARD will come after the REQUEST is made through the REVELATION of your belief. God will bring our request to pass when we believe Him according to our FAITH. Through praying prophetically you are SEEING what you SAY before it actually SHOWS UP. Now take at least (3) minutes and release a prophetic prayer right now.

"Lord God, seal each Prophetic prayer released right now and give success, strength, patience, and power to the requester…AND IT IS SO IN JESUS NAME."

What Happens When Prayer Meets Praise

When we come into the knowledge of knowing how to pray and what to pray for, our PRAYER LIFE should make contact with our PRAISE. As previously stated in the introduction of this book, I believe that when PRAYER meets PRAISE, there is a PROMISE from God that evokes Him to PRODUCE it. When PRAYER meets PRAISE at the PLACE of your PROBLEM, God will PUT a demand on PRODUCING that PARTICULAR request (I feel another shout stirring in my spirit). Your PRAYER RELEASES THE REQUEST, but it's your PRAISE THAT SEALS IT. The scripture to back up this theory is found in **"Acts 12:5, 12-16 (KJV)**, *"(5) Peter therefore was kept in prison: but prayer was made without ceasing of the church unto God for him. (12) And when he had considered the thing, he came to the house of Mary the mother of John, whose surname was Mark; where many were gathered together praying. (13) And as Peter knocked at the door of the gate, a damsel came to hearken, named Rhoda. (14) And when she knew Peter's voice, she opened not the gate for gladness, but ran in, and told how Peter stood before the gate. (15) And they said unto her, Thou art mad. But she constantly affirmed that it was even so. Then said they, It is his angel. (16) But Peter continued knocking: and when they had opened the door, and saw him, they were astonished."* This is the story of Peter, who is in prison and the church is praying for his release. WHILE they were praying, God releases what they are praying for, but because they don't see it, they kept praying.

Let me pause for a moment right here. If you're going to pray to God for Him to release something to you, you have to trust it, believe it, and expect it to happen. Just because it hasn't been revealed to you yet, it doesn't mean it hasn't been released. God responds to your request when you release it from your lips, but it's your belief in His promise to produce that will cause your request to be revealed. **"Matthew 21:22 (KJV)**, *"And all things, whatsoever ye shall ask in prayer, believing, ye shall receive."* This kind of REVELATION becomes MANIFESTATION when praise is in OPERATION. (That's something to shout about right there) Now, back to **Acts 12**. The people are still praying for Peter's release, but it's not until a little girl by the name of Rhoda goes to the door. Upon hearing the sound of Peter's voice, she runs back to the people who are praying and begins to praise God for the release (so intensely) she forgets to open the door. Here's the divine revelation of the text. Sometimes you've got to RELEASE a SHOUT at the gate before God will REVEAL you have SOMETHING at the door. *Here's where you insert an expectancy "IT'S AT THE GATE praise!"

Remember this People of God, FAITH is the place that stands between your PRAYER REQUEST and your PRAISE REPORT. So when you pray, believing in what He promised is what evokes God to produce it. The Bible says in **"Hebrews 10:23 (KJV)**, *"Let us hold fast the profession of our faith without wavering; (for he is faithful that promised)."* God did not and will not waiver on His Word, so you must trust it and Him. If you really want God to produce His promise in your life, after you pray, seal it with praise. We were taught as kids that "prayer is the key to the Kingdom and it's our faith that unlocks the door." I BELIEVE in that theory. However, I believe that there's more to that theory, I'm led to believe that if prayer is the key and faith unlocks the door, then praise reveals what's on the other side of the door. Do you need another example? How about **Acts 16:25, 26 (KJV)** that says, *"And at midnight Paul and Silas prayed, and sang praises unto God: and the prisoners heard them. And suddenly there was a great earthquake, so that the foundations of the prison were shaken: and immediately all the doors were opened, and every one's bands* *were loosed."* In this text, we learn that when prayer and praise meet at the place of a problem, God will shake things up so He can reveal (open doors) and release (bands loosed) for all those who believe. Now, that's good news to shout about right there!

By connecting your prayer and praise together, with faith, God is prompt to bring about the promise. When you know in your heart and spirit that what He promised is coming, you lift up a praise as God is producing it! I like to call this theory the STOP, DROP, and ROLL PRAISE. What is that? Well, I'm glad you asked. It's when you STOP right where you are, DROP everything you're doing and let PRAISES ROLL from your lips. Particularly, when you praise God for what you prayed about, He purposely has it delivered in the season you need it. The Bible says in **Romans 4:20, 21 (NASB)**, *"Yet, with respect to the promise of God, he did not waver in unbelief but grew strong in faith, giving glory to God, and being fully assured that what God had promised, He was able also to perform."* In other words, what was promised to Abraham came to pass because he did not waver while God worked things out for him. For us, this means that as long as we WORRY, it delays the hand of God's WORK. Encourage yourself and shout, "BE PATIENT AND PRAISE HIM!"

Remember this: whatever you ASK God for is only ACCEPTED when it's followed up by an ACTION that ALIGNS itself with what was ASKED. That's why Paul said in **Philippians 4:6 (KJV)**, *"Be careful for nothing; but in every thing by prayer and supplication with thanksgiving let your requests be made known unto God."* There must be a VISIBLE ACTION that follows your VERBAL ASKING. When we fail to praise God after we've prayed, we basically fail to complete the work needed to produce the request. David says in **Psalms 141:2 (KJV)**, *"Let my prayer be set forth before thee as incense; and the lifting up of my hands as the evening sacrifice."* David is saying in this scripture that when prayer is done effectively it gets God's attention, but praise, when it's done after prayer, moves God's authority. Wait a minute…the perfect example of this principle is Jesus on the cross in **Matthew 27:46 (KJV)**: *"And about the ninth hour Jesus cried (prayed) with a loud voice, saying, Eli, Eli, lama sabachthani? that is to say, My God, my God, why hast thou forsaken me?"* Jesus in this passage, released, what I believe, was a prayer to get God's ATTENTION and felt like many of us at times, as if God had ABANDONED Him. But if you keep reading the text, you'll discover in **Matthew 27:50 (KJV)** that *"Jesus, when he had cried again with a loud voice, yielded up the ghost* **(the spirit moved)**."When we see Jesus praying it was to get God's ATTENTION, but the moment He prayed again, it moved God's AUTHORITY. I don't know about you but I'd rather have the AUTHORITY of God than the ATTENTION of God. Here's why. In **Luke 19:1-5 (KJV)**, there is a man by the name of Zacchaeus, who was a chief tax collector. He wanted to see Jesus but could not because of the crowd. If you notice, the crowd was only around Him, but didn't need anything from Him. However, Zacchaeus, who wanted something from Jesus ran and climbed a sycamore tree, not to get His attention but to move His authority. Here's another example. In **Mark 5:25-34 (KJV)**, there was a woman who suffered with an issue of blood for 12 years and kept getting worse. When she heard Jesus was in town, she pressed her way through the crowd of people who were with Jesus and didn't need anything from Him. She pressed her way through them to touch the hem of His garment thus receiving her healing. She did not do this for attention, she did this to move His authority. *My God Today! I think I'm shouting way too much in this book* JESUS THE CHRIST, THANK YOU FOR YOUR AUTHORITY!"

When we were little, we used to sing a song in the Christian church entitled, "I WILL TRUST IN THE LORD" and one of the verses says, "I'M GONNA WATCH, FIGHT, and PRAY." Now, I'm not stomping against the tradition of the song, but I do have one problem with it. Technically and scripturally, we're not told to fight anyway. Paul tells the church at

Ephesus that our war is not to be fought with PEOPLE, but with the POWER OF PRAYER. Conversely, the main purpose of the Armour of God is not for us to STRUGGLE WITH who's attacking us, but for us to STAND WHILE we're being attacked. **Ephesians 6:12-14a (KJV)** says, *"For we wrestle* **(to engage to contend with)** *not against flesh and blood, but against principalities, against powers, against the rulers of the darkness of this world, against spiritual wickedness in high places. Wherefore take unto you the whole armor of God, that ye may be able to WITHSTAND in the evil day, and having done all, to STAND."* Our whole survival should be based upon our FORTITUDE, and not how well we FIGHT. Tell yourself, "STOP FIGHTING AND STAND!"

Let's continue. Now, after Paul reveals the whole Armor of God, he then shares with us how to fight with that armor. His resolution of spiritual fighting, found in **Ephesians 6:18 (KJV)** says for us to, *"Pray always with all prayer and supplication in the Spirit, and watching thereunto with all perseverance and supplication for all saints."* Basically, he's suggesting for us to not FIGHT AND PRAY, but to FIGHT IN PRAYER, and by fighting in prayer, we place God on the battlefield to fight on our behalf. Here are a few scriptures to back up that theory.

The psalmist says in **Psalms 46:7-11 (KJV)**, *"The Lord of hosts is with us; the God of Jacob is our refuge. Selah. Come, behold the works of the Lord, what desolations he hath made in the earth. He maketh wars to cease unto the end of the earth; he breaketh the bow, and cutteth the spear in sunder; he burneth the chariot in the fire. Be still, and know that I am God: I will be exalted among the heathen, I will be exalted in the earth. The Lord of hosts is with us; the God of Jacob is our refuge. Selah."*

God told Jehoshaphat and the inhabitants of Jerusalem and Judah in **2 Chronicles 20:15-18 (KJV)**, *"And he said, Hearken ye, all Judah, and ye inhabitants of Jerusalem, and thou king Jehoshaphat, Thus saith the Lord unto you, Be not afraid nor dismayed by reason of this great multitude; for the battle is not yours, but God's. Tomorrow go ye down against them: behold, they* *come up by the cliff of Ziz; and ye shall find them at the end of the brook, before the wilderness of Jeruel. Ye shall not need to fight in this battle: set yourselves, stand ye still, and see the salvation of the Lord with you, O Judah and Jerusalem: fear not, nor be dismayed; tomorrow go out against them: for the Lord will be with you."* In other words, we're NOT told to WATCH, FIGHT, and PRAY. However, we are told to WATCH, PRAY, and PRAISE. Paul says in **Colossians 4:2 (KJV)**, to *"Continue in prayer, and watch in the same with thanksgiving."* Let your PRAYER meet your PRAISE and watch God PERFORM it in your life.

How to Identify Your Purpose in God's Plan

Since we now understand how to prophetically pray and how prayer and praise works for us, we can dive into the understanding of how to identify our purpose in God's plan through prayer. In order to do that, we must first identify what that purpose is and where it fits in God's plan for our lives.

What is PURPOSE? PURPOSE: the reason for the existence of something or the intention of a desired result, goal, or end. As stated, PURPOSE is the reason why you're here on earth and the accomplishment of what you're expected, intended, destined and/or determined to do. It should be the PURPOSE of every believer to fulfill the work God sent you here to accomplish. Jesus himself said in **John 9:4, 5 (KJV)**, *"I must work the works of him that sent me, while it is day: the night cometh, when no man can work. As long as I am in the world, I am the light of the world."* He identified His purpose by declaring that He was and still is the light and that the world, through Him, would be able to see clearly. He also reminded us in **John 3:17 (KJV)**, *"For God sent not his Son into the world to condemn the world; but that the world through him might be saved."* Jesus was sent here to fulfill an assignment given by His father which meant He had a promise in fulfilling His purpose.

We all have a purpose to fulfill no matter what the age, the same as Jesus. God has given us a Divine assignment to accomplish which is identified as our purpose in life. Even from the beginning of time, it was the original intent of God to give man PURPOSE before He gave him POSITION and POWER. Don't believe me? The bible says in

Genesis 1:26-28 (KJV), *"And God said, Let us make man in our image, after our likeness:* **(the plan)** *and let them have dominion over* **(the purpose)** *the fish of the sea, and over the fowl of the air, and over the cattle, and over all the earth, and over every creeping thing that creepeth upon the earth. So God created man in his own image, in the image of God created he him; male and female created he them. And God blessed them, and God said unto them, Be fruitful, and multiply, and replenish the earth, and subdue it: and have dominion over the fish of the sea, and over the fowl of the air, and over every living thing that moveth upon the earth."* **Genesis 2:7-9, 15 (KJV)**, *"And the Lord God formed man of the dust of the ground, and breathed into his nostrils the breath of life; and man became a living soul* **(power)**. *And the Lord God planted a garden eastward in Eden, and there he put the man whom he had formed. And out of the ground made the Lord God to grow every tree that is pleasant to the sight, and good for food; the tree of life also in the midst of the garden, and the tree of knowledge of good and evil. And the Lord God took the man, and put him into the garden of Eden to dress it and to keep it* **(position)**." This suggests to us, that God's intended plan for man was to purpose him with power, then position him in a place where that power could be displayed. God created you with Divine purpose, gave you power, and positioned you in a place where that power He gave you can be used daily in every area of your life.

I have more scripture to back me up found in **Jeremiah 1:5 (KJV)**, *"Before I formed thee in the belly I knew thee; and before thou camest forth out of the womb I sanctified thee, and I ordained thee a Prophet unto the nations."* God ordained us before we were born with power and purpose for doing Kingdom work. This means "YOU'RE NOT JUST HERE ON PURPOSE, YOUR HERE FOR PURPOSE." In order to make an impact in the lives of others you have to understand God has given you a Divine assignment. You were not sent here to be ordinary, plain, or laid back. God chose you and set you apart to be a blessing to others. The Bible says in **1 Peter 2:9 (KJV)**, *"But ye are a chosen generation, a royal priesthood,* an holy nation, a peculiar people; that ye should shew forth the praises of him who hath called you out of darkness into his marvelous light." God is using your life to bring light to His promises over your life and others, which means that you've been divinely picked on with an ordained purpose to fulfill that divine promise.

As a child of God, I've discovered that you can have promise, yet not understand your purpose in order to fulfill that promise. Why? Because purpose is your intent, your determination, your motivation, your fire, your zeal, and/or your passion to reach your destiny. That's why David said in **Psalms 51:12 (KJV)**, *"Restore unto me the joy of thy salvation; and uphold me with thy free spirit."* David was simply saying (paraphrased), "Lord, give me back my passion and purpose so that I can reach my place of promise." Let me drop this in your spirit. You cannot be deterred from your destiny or lose what's promised to you except if you rebel and turn away from the saving power of God. Even though destiny is already predetermined and the promise of a prosperous life is already in the plans of God, if we fail to follow His guidelines, we delay God's delivery of fulfilling that destiny in our lives. For the Lord says in **Jeremiah 29:11 (NIV)**, *"For I know the plans I have for you," declares the Lord, "plans to prosper you and not to harm you, plans to give you hope and a future."* God's plans for your life are already determined, but it's up to you to identify your purpose in His predestined plan.

I hear you asking me, "So, how do I identify my purpose in God's plans for my life?" Well, I'm glad you asked. You identify your purpose through: PATTERNS and PASSIONS.

PATTERNS: (repetitive occurrences throughout the course of life)

Example: As a little boy, I always found myself around preachers. At the time, I thought it was fascinating watching the way they preached, not realizing that they were watering a seed that was already planted in me before I was born. Those patterns that I began to mimic sparked a passion in me to fulfill the purpose for my life.

So, PATTERNS are FASCINATIONS (to arouse the interest or curiosity of; to attract and hold the attention of by a unique gift or power) of your PASSIONS.

PASSION: (a strong desire or feeling to accomplish something in life)

Example: During the time I was developing and growing spiritually, those patterns that I had become accustomed to, watching those preachers preach, turned from a mere fascination to a moving fire. I noticed that what was being poured into me was becoming more powerful than what was being pulled out of me, which ignited my passion for my purpose. So, I stopped mimicking what I SAW and started managing, researching, studying, exercising, and training myself to understand what God SAID was inside of me. That which started out as a FASCINATION is now a FIRE shut up in my bones like it was for the Prophet Jeremiah. **(reference Jeremiah 20:9)**.

* PASSIONS are FIRES (a burning desire, fervor, and enthusiasm; an intense devotion to do something) erupted out of your PURPOSE.*

Those seed sowing patterns and the watering of your passion make up your God-given purpose. Without that seed being sown by the Spirit and without having that seed watered by the Word, which activates your works, your purpose will miss the time, season, and opportunity to be fruitful. **"Ecclesiastes 3:1 (KJV)**, *"To everything, there is a season, and a time to every purpose under the heaven."* This scripture states that purpose has a specific time and season for it to be fruitful and fulfill the destined plan for your life. All that means is that you cannot die until what you were purposed to do gets done because God's hand is on his plan for your life. The Bible says in **Isaiah 14:26, 27 (KJV)**, *"This is the purpose that is purposed upon the whole earth: and this is the hand that is stretched out upon all the nations. For the Lord of hosts hath purposed, and who shall disannul it? and his hand is stretched out, and who shall turn it back".* Simply put, God's purpose has already been placed inside of you, so you would have to literally remove God's hand in order to cancel his plan over your life. GOOD LUCK WITH THAT.

In order to assist you with fulfilling your purpose in life, God will give you visions as well as valley experiences that will help you discover and develop your purpose. When you have a VISION, you must remember that there will always be a VALLEY experience connected to it. **Isaiah 22:1 (KJV)** says, *"The burden of the valley of vision. What aileth thee now, that thou art wholly gone up to the housetops?"* Therefore, we have to learn how to trust our VISION and accept the TRIALS that comes along with it. Always remember that people are connected to your VISION, not to your VALLEY. You can not expect everyone to understand what you're GOING THROUGH in the VALLEY, because they aren't the ones assigned to it. ONE MORE TIME for those who missed it. People aren't assigned to your spiritual birthing process in the VALLEY, according to **Isaiah 22:5 (KJV)**, *"For it is a day of trouble, and of treading down, and of perplexity by the Lord God of hosts in the valley of vision, breaking down the walls, and of crying to the mountains."* People are assigned to only believe in the production of your VISION. They will not sacrifice as much as you will. So, stop trying to make them COSIGN your CALLING or VALIDATE your VISION. They will never understand the VALLEY you had to go through to get it. I don't know if this will help you or not, but that's what the VALLEY experience is for. It will bring VALIDATION to your VOCATION. David wrote in **Psalms 23:4 (KJV)**, *"Yea, though I walk through the valley of the shadow of death, I will fear no evil: for thou art with me; thy rod* **(used for correcting)** *and thy staff* **(used for caressing)** *they comfort me."* Your valley experiences will bring divine correction and caressing to your calling. God anointed your VISION with a VOICE, so stop trying to make your VALLEY be the SPOKESMAN for your VISION. In other words, we ought not speak only from where we are in the VALLEY (our pains, problems, trials, and trouble), but mostly from where we are going in the VISION (healing, strength, peace of mind, blessings of God). Let your VISION speak for itself. And even though there's a BURDEN to it, wait for the BENEFITS of it. It'll be the BEST THING to ever happen to you.

How to Stop The Enemy From Stopping Your Prayers

*N*ow that you understand how to pray, what it means to prophetically pray, what happens when your prayer and praise comes together, and how to identify your purpose in God's plan, you must now learn the part the enemy plays in trying to stop that prayer from being productive in your life. Paul said in **2 Corinthians 2:11 (KJV)**, *"Lest Satan should get an advantage of us: for we are not ignorant of his devices."* It is vitally important to understand the enemy's role concerning our prayer requests. It is the strategic plan and purpose of the enemy to steal your requests, hinder your response, and destroy your reception. He realizes that your PLACE OF PEACE is stuck between your PRAYER REQUEST and your PRAISE REPORT. So, his ultimate task is to hold up any progress whether it's the petition or the promise. Our petitions have to be carefully and faithfully thought out, because he's known as *"the prince of the power of the air"* according to **Ephesians 2:2 (KJV)**. In order to stop him from intercepting our petitions and delaying the promises of God, we may consider doing prayer in different ways and start using another method such as writing them down.

The bible has stated you don't have to pray openly or even out loud on every occasion that you spend time with God. Our requests can be written and non-verbal and here are a few scriptures to back up that theory.

"Matthew 6:6 (KJV), *"But thou, when thou prayest, enter into thy closet, and when thou hast shut thy door, pray to thy Father which is in secret; and thy Father which seeth in secret shall reward thee openly."*

This scripture suggests that whatever you pray for PRIVATELY, God will respond and reward you with it PUBLICLY!

"Mark 11:24 (KJV), *"Therefore I say unto you, What things soever ye desire, when ye pray, believe that ye receive them, and ye shall have them."*

This clearly declares that whatever we desire when we pray, as long as we believe it, we shall have them. In other words, it never said that you have to pray openly, but it's through your heart's desire and belief in God that He will bring those things you desire to pass.

"Luke 11:9, 10 (KJV), *"And I say unto you, Ask, and it shall be given you; seek, and ye shall find; knock, and it shall be opened unto you. For every one that asketh receiveth; and he that seeketh findeth, and to him that knocketh it shall be opened."*

Even though this scripture says to ask, it doesn't say how to ask. God is, and has always been, a God of specifics. So, if it was specifically meant for us to ask openly, He would have directly said for us to ask verbally, but because He didn't say how to ask, we can conclude that no matter how we ask anything, if we believe, we will receive.

Remember this People of God, the devil used to be the "anointed cherub" named Lucifer (which means "son of the morning"), who was stationed over the Angelic voices in Heaven. He was specially created by God according to **Colossians 1:16, 17 (KJV)**, *"For by him were all things created, that are in heaven, and that are in earth, visible and invisible, whether they be thrones, or dominions, or principalities, or powers: all things were created by him, and for him: And he is before all things, and by him all things consist."* He had the word, viols, and musical instrumentation placed in him, according to **Ezekiel 28:12-15 (KJV)**, *"Thou hast been in Eden the garden of God; every precious stone was thy covering, the sardius, topaz, and the diamond, the beryl, the onyx, and the jasper, the sapphire, the emerald, and the carbuncle, and gold: the workmanship of thy tabrets and of thy pipes was prepared in thee in the day that thou wast created. Thou art the anointed cherub that covereth; and I have set thee so: thou wast upon the holy mountain of*

God; thou hast walked up and down in the midst of the stones of fire. Thou wast perfect in thy ways from the day that thou wast created, till iniquity was found in thee." This signifies to me that he was and still is a skilled musician with a trained ear to hear words and lyrical sounds. His ONLY assignment was to set an atmosphere in Heaven with his gift, so that God could be glorified. However, according to **Isaiah 14:11-14 (KJV)**, *"Thy pomp is brought down to the grave, and the noise of thy viols: the worm is spread under thee, and the worms cover thee. How art thou fallen from heaven, O Lucifer, son of the morning! How art thou cut down to the ground, which didst weaken the nations! For thou hast said in thine heart, I will ascend into heaven, I will exalt my throne above the stars of God: I will sit also upon the mount of the congregation, in the sides of the north: I will ascend above the heights of the clouds; I will be like the most High."* He gets arrogant, prideful and loses his place, his power, and his position in Heaven causing him to no longer be heard, according to **Ezekiel 26:13 (KJV)**, *"And I will cause the noise of thy songs to cease; and the sound of thy harps shall be no more heard."* Consequently, God removes him from his assignment in Heaven of setting an atmosphere for His glory and replaces him with us. He creates man from the dust of the earth, giving man his assignment to set an atmosphere for God to get the glory. Hence the reason for Satan entering into a serpent, according to **Genesis 3:1 (KJV)**, so he could use craftiness to convince the creation to turn against the plans of the Creator.

It's important that you understand Lucifer is mad at God because he's no longer in Heaven doing what he was created to do. The Glory he was removed from, he was also replaced by the sons of God. (Sorry, but I found another place to shout and give God the praise. Thank you Lord for giving me access to your GLORY!! God gave the assignment of a worship leader to man and every time man begins to worship God, it becomes an immediate reminder to Lucifer, who is now Satan (after his fall from Heaven his nature and name changes), of who he was and the place where he once occupied. When we as created worshippers begin to release a sound of worship from our lips, it basically reminds the devil that he was REMOVED to be REPLACED. Since he cannot attack the Creator (God), he attacks His creation (man) with permitted chaos and confusion in order to get the creation to turn against the Creator. That's Satan's only way of attempting to triumph over God who he knows he can't defeat. I double dare you to put this book down right now and begin to worship the Lord your God. Worship Him not for what He does, but for who He is. *Worship Praise Break* Thank you Lord for being our

LORD
SAVIOR
REDEEMER
HEALER
PROVIDER
PROTECTOR
WAYMAKER
MIRACLE WORKER
PROMISE KEEPER
DELIVERER
SHELTER

OUR EVERYTHING. THANK YOU, LORD!! HALLELUJAH!! GLORY TO YOUR NAME!! JESUS CHRIST...MY GOD TODAY... HOW GREAT THOU ART...HOLY ARE YOU LORD...whew!

I almost forgot I was writing a book. Ladies and Gentlemen, I want you to know that there really is something about the name Jesus. I tell you that it's the sweetest name I know. There's SO MUCH POWER in His name. Now, I understand why demons are TERRIFIED by the name and we are TRIUMPHANT because of it. Ok, I'm back...LORD, WE BLESS YOUR NAME!! Hallelujah to your name!! Glory to your name Jesus!!

So I hear you asking me, "But how and why does he attack our requests?" Well, I'm glad you asked. Here's how you know. Have you ever noticed that whatever you openly ask God for, seems to always get attacked and never come into manifestation? For example, every time you pray for FINANCIAL BLESSINGS to come into your life, it's normally in your finances where the Lord grants permission for you to be attacked by the enemy, according to **Job 1:6-12 (KJV)**, *"Now there was a day when the sons of God came to present themselves before the LORD, and Satan came also among them. And the LORD said unto Satan, Whence comest thou? Then Satan answered the LORD, and said, From going to and fro in the earth, and from walking up and down in it. And the LORD said unto Satan, Hast thou considered my servant Job, that there is none like him in the earth, a perfect and an upright man, one that feareth God, and escheweth evil? Then Satan answered the LORD, and said, Doth Job fear God for nought? Hast not thou made a hedge about him, and about his house, and about all that he hath on every side? thou hast blessed the work of his hands, and his substance is increased in the land. But put forth thine hand now, and touch all that he hath, and he will curse thee to thy face. And the LORD said unto Satan, Behold, all that he hath is in thy power; only upon himself put not forth thine hand. So Satan went forth from the presence of the LORD."* This suggests to me that if the enemy is ATTACKING you, it's mainly because God gave the APPROVAL. In other words, God CONSIDERED you for the CHAOS, because He has CONTROL over his CHAOS and will take CARE of you in the process. Here's a great place to pause for a praise break. Glory!! Hallelujah!!

Now back to our regularly scheduled programming. **(smile)** When we start making our requests to God, because Satan was and still is trained to hear, he listens for keywords such as, family, faith, finance, mind, and heart in the requests during our prayer time and asks for permission to attack them. After hearing those requests, he then sends satanic sabotages to strategically hold up and hold back all of our petitions and tries to stall out all of God's promises made to us. Keep in mind that he's "the prince of the power of the air" which means strategically Satan is set in a position to hinder all those things designed to bring true help, hope, and healing to our lives. Even though this scripture is not contextually about the devil, the content of this scripture is the ideal plan of the devil. The Bible says in **John 10:10 (KJV)**, *"The thief cometh not, but for to steal* **(focus = strength)**, *and to kill* **(fruit = seed)**, *and to destroy* **(faith = salvation)***: I am come that they* **(strength, seed, and salvation)** *might have life, and that they might have it more abundantly."* This is great news to the believer that no matter what the enemy is trying to do, Jesus will always override the enemy's plan so you can live abundantly.

People of God, despite what the devil is permitted to do, we've been given a divine weapon in the angelic authority of the Archangel Michael, the warring angel as mentioned in **Revelations 12:7-9 (KJV)**, *"And there was war in heaven: Michael and his angels fought against the dragon; and the dragon fought and his angels, And prevailed not; neither was their place found any more in heaven. And the great dragon was cast out, that old serpent, called the Devil, and Satan, which deceiveth the whole world: he was cast out into the earth, and his angels were cast out with him."* He is released at our request to defend our petitions and free up God's promises for us to receive. **Daniel 10:11-13 (KJV)** tells us: *"He* **(Gabriel, the messenger angel)** *said, "Daniel, you who are highly esteemed, consider carefully the words I am about to speak to you, and stand up, for I have now been sent to you." And when he said this to me, I stood up trembling. Then he continued, "Do not be afraid, Daniel. Since the first day that you set your mind to gain understanding and to humble yourself before your God, your words were heard, and I have come in response to them. But the prince of the Persian kingdom* **(Satan)** *resisted me twenty-one days. Then Michael, one of the chief princes, came to help me,* *because I was detained there with the king of Persia."* This text simply suggests to us that, the moment we request something from God, He releases the answer at the time it is requested. However, Satan gets in position to disrupt and derail what God released, in the hopes that his holding the blessing hostage, will ultimately cause us to lose faith in God. "Silly Rabbit!" Satan doesn't realize that holding up the blessing of a true believer only encourages that person to trust God even more. I don't know about you, but I TRUST GOD TOO MUCH FOR ME TO MISS MY BLESSING!!

Not only is Michael an angelic weapon, but our written prayer requests are weapons to stop the enemy from blocking us and receiving. Remember, when God created Lucifer He placed in him the Word. For example in **Matthew 4:1-11 / Luke 4:1-13 (KJV)**, Satan tries to use the word placed in him to overtake and overthrow the beginning of Jesus Ministry and mission. However, Jesus' response is vitally important, because He shows us how to counter-attack the plots and plans of the enemy without opening our mouths with enticing words or phrases. Jesus said, "IT IS WRITTEN.." which signifies to me that evidently the devil cannot read, and if he cannot read then when I start writing down my requests and petitions, making them known unto God, he cannot attack what he does not hear. As a matter of fact, he waits to hear what you request of God so he can launch an all-out attack on that very thing.

Let's review. So far, we've been told that the devil was once an "anointed cherub" in Heaven assigned over Heaven's worship to God. He was so puffed up with pride, thought he was equal with The Most High God. He wanted power, as well as an image like God, which got him expelled from Eternity. SMH...WRONG MOVE!! He gets immediately banished from Heaven by God, falls to the earth according to **Luke 10:18 (KJV)**, *"And he said unto them, I beheld Satan as lightning fall from heaven."* He landed in the place where the Trinity **(God the Father, Jesus the Son, and The Holy Spirit)** decides to make man in God's image and after His own likeness. Of course, this upsets the Devil, Satan the Serpent, and he revengefully attacks God's CREATION in order for them to turn against the CREATOR, according to **Revelations 2:10 (KJV)**, *"Fear none of those things which thou shalt suffer: behold, the devil shall cast some of you into prison, that ye may be tried; and ye shall have tribulation ten days: be thou faithful unto death, and I will give thee a crown of life."*

When scriptures are used in your requests to God, the devil launches an all-out attack in order to weaken your faith and trust in the promise of it coming to pass. There will be times when you can't get a verbal prayer out because the cares of life have overtaken you. It's at this time you may apply the literal and faithful method found in **Habakkuk 2:2, 3 (KJV)**, *"And the Lord answered me, and said, Write the VISION, and make it plain upon tables, that he may run that readeth it. For the vision is yet for an appointed time, but at the end it shall speak, and not lie: though it tarry, wait for it; because it will surely come, it will not tarry."* In other words, when we start to write down the VISION **(the act or power of anticipating that which will or may come to be)**, making it PLAIN **(simple)** upon the tables, but at the end of writing IT **(the vision, the request, the desire, or the need)**, IT **(the vision, the request, the desire, or the need)** will SPEAK **(open request)** and what you've written will not TARRY **(delay or be tardy in acting or coming)** but IT **(the vision, the request, the desire, or the need)** will COME TO PASS **(manifest)**.

As a matter of fact, when you openly pray, don't mention the vision, the request, the need nor desire out loud, but say to the Father openly to "BLESS THIS, COVER THIS, MANIFEST THIS, TOUCH THIS, ANOINT THIS, BRING THIS TO PASS, INCREASE THIS." will confuse the enemy because he's trying to hear that specific thing you need so that he can block and stop it. And by saying the word, "THIS," he's going to have a hard time trying to figure out what "THIS" is and how to attack it and you. So the next time you need something special from God and since the devil can't read, start writing those prayer requests down. And when you pray, don't mention what you've written, just shout, "THIS" which will release everything you need from Heaven. That's how you stop the enemy from stopping your prayers. I believe now is the perfect time to release another shout of praise! Hallelujah to your name Lord God! Glory!

Watch What You Release and How You Release It

Because you now understand the strategic plan of the enemy and how to counter attack it, it is vitally important to watch what you release and the attitude in which you release it. The Bible says in **Matthew 7:7, 8 (KJV)**, *"Ask, and it shall be given you; seek, and ye shall find; knock, and it shall be opened unto you: For every one that asketh receiveth; and he that seeketh findeth; and to him that knocketh it shall be opened."* This means that whatever you request from God, you can expect to come to pass. For example, if I keep releasing into the atmosphere that I'm HEALED, then my faith releases HEALING into my life. If I loose into the atmosphere that I'm BLESSED, then my faith releases BLESSINGS into my life. However, if I confess into the atmosphere that I'm BROKE, then the faith I release is not in line with God's Word, but in being BROKE and suffering lack.

In **James 4:3 (KJV)**, the Bible states *"Ye ask, and receive not, because ye ask amiss* **(not in the proper or right condition or attitude; wrong motives)**, *that ye may consume it upon your lusts."* In essence, we basically need to be careful about what we request or release into the atmosphere for God to deliver into our lives. Here are a few scriptures to back up this theory.

"Luke 6:45 (KJV) - "A good man out of the good treasure of his heart bringeth forth that which is good; and an evil man out of the evil treasure of his heart bringeth forth that which is evil: for of the abundance of the heart his mouth speaketh."

This scripture teaches us that we must be careful in what we release out of our mouths and from our hearts. The good in us will produce good things for and around us, but the evil in us will generate evil things to manifest in our lives. Because out of our heart flows the issues of life we have to do a heart check before we release things in the atmosphere. In other words, watch what you release!"

"John 14:13, 14 (KJV) - *"And whatsoever ye shall ask in my name, that will I do, that the Father may be glorified in the Son. If ye shall ask anything in my name, I will do it."*

When you pray in Jesus' name, if you believe in WHO you're petitioning and WHAT is being requested, the Lord promised to bring it to pass, not for you to be glorified, but for God to be glorified through your belief in His Son. He tells us to ask and it will be done. As stated in the following scripture **"Psalms 37:5 (KJV)** - *"Commit thy way unto the Lord; trust also in him; and he shall bring it to pass."*

This declares that whatever you commit to or request in faith, God will make it covenant and manifest it. God is making a COVENANT {**a solemn agreement or promise**} out of whatever you COMMIT {**submit; to present**} to Him. So be careful of what you commit to because it is destined to come to pass. The bible says in **Deuteronomy 23:21-23 (NIV)**, *"If you make a vow to the LORD your God, do not be slow to pay it, for the LORD your God will certainly demand it of you and you will be guilty of sin. But if you refrain from making a vow, you will not be guilty. Whatever your lips utter you must be sure to do, because you made your vow freely to the LORD your God with your own mouth."*

You should not only watch what you release, but you need to watch how you release it. What is your attitude in receiving what you're requesting from God? Is your attitude conducive to helping the manifestation of your request or is it hindering it? If your ATTITUDE is not right, then your ALTITUDE will not be right, simply because your PHYSICAL ATTITUDE is what shifts your SPIRITUAL ALTITUDE in manifestation. Scripture declares in **Philippians 2:3 (KJV),**

"Let nothing be done through strife **(bitterness)** or vainglory **(too much self-pride)**; but in lowliness **(humility)** of mind let each esteem other better than themselves." Nothing you do or pray for should be requested in a negative attitude form, but in a humble mindset expecting a prosperous outcome.

The Bible also says in **Philippians 1:4-6 (KJV)**, *"Always in every prayer of mine for you all making request with joy, For your fellowship in the gospel from the first day until now; Being confident of this very thing, that he which hath begun a good work in you will perform it until the day of Jesus Christ."* So when you pray or make your request to God, the attitude you have will bring the good work of God into manifestation through His son, Jesus which lives in you. So, the next time you release something into the atmosphere, be mindful that what you release on earth is being released in Heaven. Remember, the Bible says in **Matthew 16:19 (KJV)**, *"And I will give unto thee the keys of the kingdom of heaven: and whatsoever thou shalt bind* **(to hold and/or restrict; to lock)** *on earth shall be bound* **(held and restricted)** *in heaven: and whatsoever thou shalt loose* **(to set free and/or release; to unlock)** *on earth shall be loosed* **(freed and released)** *in heaven."* People of God, be careful what you release in this season because it will be loosed from Heaven into your life.

Now that you know how to attack the enemy that's attacking you and how to be careful in what you release in the atmosphere, it's time to declare some Prophetic prayers of power into, around, and over your life because of everything connected to your life. I've been charged and commissioned by God to release a different way to prophetically pray in alphabetical order. So, I encourage you with elation, excitement, and enthusiasm to PROPHETICALLY PRAY these prayers of promise in and around your life on purpose and then release a SHOUT OF PRAISE to seal what you've spoken into the atmosphere. Let's go to work!

"The (A) Prayer of Power"

1 Thessalonians 5:22 - "ABSTAIN from
ALL APPEARANCE of evil."

ALMIGHTY ALPHA, ALLOW us ALL to be in AWE AS we ACCESS your ANOINTING AROUND our ATMOSPHERES. We ACTIVATE with ANTICIPATION AND APPRECIATION your AGELESS ADDITIONS, AS we ATTEMPT to ADORE your AWESOMENESS in our ACTIVE ASSIGNMENTS. We ACCEPT ACCOUNTABILITY for our ACTIONS, we're ADDICTED to your AGAPE love towards us AND we AIM to ASSERT our ABLED ACCOMPLISHMENTS under your AFFIRMATION knowing that no AMOUNT of time is ADEQUATE to ACKNOWLEDGE ALL of your AMAZING ACTS. We ASK for your ASSISTANCE in ASSASSINATING our ACCUSER AND ATTACKER AND ALSO in ACCURATELY ARRESTING our ANGER, AGGRESSION, ARROGANCE, ADDICTIONS, AGGRAVATIONS AND AGITATIONS and we ADJUST ourselves to be on one ACCORD with you. ACE the ALTERATIONS of our ATTITUDES in AGREEABLE ADORATION towards you AND we're not AFRAID to ALIGN ourselves AFTER your AFFLICTIONS. We ADAMANTLY ADVANCE in your ABSOLUTE AUTHORITY and ANCHOR our ABILITIES in the ANSWER of your AUTHENTIC ATTRIBUTES AND ABUNDANCE. AWESOME ADMINISTRATOR, we AUTOMATICALLY AWAKE AND become AVAILABLE to you... AND it is so!

BAILEY-OLOGY BLESSING:

Now Father, I seal this prophetic prayer of power in the Blood of Jesus and in the fresh wind of the Holy Spirit. I speak confirmation and clarity into every person who reads and believes this prayer and who releases it for others to enjoy and encounter you personally. Bring divine order to it, prosperity to it and manifest it IMMEDIATELY as we celebrate you in everything we do. Shift the atmosphere and align everything in your Word. AND IT IS SO in the mighty, majestic and marvelous name of Jesus, Oh Lord and Savior, we shout, pray, and celebrate. Amen!

"The (B) Prayer of Power"

> John 20:31 - "Then said Jesus to them again, Peace be unto you: as my Father hath sent me, even so send I you. But these are written, that ye might BELIEVE that Jesus is the Christ, the Son of God; and that BELIEVING ye might have life through his name."

BONJOUR BLESSED God, thanks for BREATHING on every BORN-again BELIEVER with a BUFFET of BOUNTIFUL BLESSINGS. I BESEECH you to BREAK down every BARRIER of those who have BEEN BROKEN, BITTER, BATTERED, and BRUISED as well as BESTOW the BIGGEST BREAKTHROUGH ever BIRTHED through your BELOVED Son, Jesus. We're making sure to BEWARE of the BETRAYAL of the BEAST named BEELZEBUB, BUT stand BOLDLY to BUST open and BLACKEN his BROOD of BEWITCHMENT BY BINDING our BELIEFS in the BROW of your BEAUTIFUL BOOK BRANDED as the BIBLE. We BEND BEYOND the BONDS of our BRAINS BAPTIZED in BELIEVING that the BABY that was BORN in BETHLEHEM will BRING us BAILS of BETTER. We BRACE for the BOOM of your BREATHTAKING BENEFITS and BASK in the BREEZE that's BREWING BRISKLY through the BRETHREN. We BOW down and BATHE in your BULKY BILLIONS as you BANDAGE our BANK accounts BACK to their BENEFICIAL BRIGHTNESS and BALANCE. BESIDES, your BEST leaves us BAFFLED and BEFUDDLED anyway so we BLESS you…And it is so!

BAILEY-OLOGY BLESSING:

Now Father, I seal this prophetic prayer of power in the Blood of Jesus and in the fresh wind of the Holy Spirit. I speak the release of your unstoppable blessings upon every reader and those they will share this with. I ask for an immediate shift in every situation of their lives and for you Oh God, to stir up every gift in their lives. I expect your Spirit to invade the place and privacy of every believer who trusts you for their next miracle. Bring them to a fruitful end in you as you bless us in the process. AND IT IS SO in the mighty, majestic and marvelous name of Jesus, our Lord and Savior, we shout, pray, and celebrate. AMEN!

"The (C) Prayer of Power"

Matthew 11:28 - "COME unto me, all ye that labor and are heavy laden, and I will give you rest."

CHRIST, we COME to you CHARMED by your CHARITY and CHARGED to CARVE your CARELESS CHARACTER into the CHAPELS of our CREATED bodies. We make a CONSCIOUS CHOICE to CHASE after your COMPANIONSHIP as you CARRY us through the CLASSES of CHRISTIANITY. We COMMAND your COMPASSIONATE CONTROL to COMMUTE us while you CONTINUE to CARESS, COMFORT and CONTAIN our CONCERNS and CUT loose the CRACKS of our CRAZINESS. We CANCEL every CHAOTIC CREATURE COMING to CONFUSE our COMMITMENT and CONTAMINATE our COVENANT with you as you CRUNCH, CRUSH and CRIPPLE the CRUSADE of Satan's CURSES. We COVER ourselves with the COMMANDMENTS and CHARISMA of our CHIEF CORNERSTONE whose CREASE we CONNECT our CREATIVITY to and whose CROSS is our CROWN. We CONCLUDE and CLOSE this COLLAGE with a CLAP of CONTINUAL CONTENTMENT and CONVENIENCED CONSIDERATION of your CARE…And it is so!

BAILEY-OLOGY BLESSING:
Now Father, I seal this prophetic prayer of power in the Blood of Jesus and in the fresh wind of the Holy Spirit. I speak countless blessings over, around and on every reader and those they share it with. Release your manifested favor and power upon their request and shower your peace

in the places of their problems. I expect a miracle, a sign, and a wonder to be unlocked and every diabolical spirit sent to hinder the process and progress, banned and blocked now. Let the Glory of the Lord be revealed in all of its splendor and grace. AND IT IS SO in the mighty, majestic and marvelous name of Jesus, our Lord and Savior, we shout, pray, and celebrate. AMEN!

"The (D) Prayer of Power"

Psalms 34:19 - "Many are the afflictions of the righteous: but the Lord DELIVERETH him out of them all."

DEAR DADDY, thank you for DAYS of DANCING like DAVID and for DIAGNOSING us with a DEBONAIR DECAL. Please DISCLOSE a DOSE of DELIVERANCE for those who are DEEMED worthy from the DISTORTION and DISTRACTION of every DEMONIC and DIABOLICAL DEMON. We DECREE and DECLARE the DISPATCH of your DESIGNED DEMOLITION team to DERAIL and DEMOLISH every DISRUPTION and DASTARDLY DEED of the DEVIL as you DISCREETLY DIRECT the DETERMINATION of our DESTINY in your DEITY. We DRIVE towards your DIVINE DIVINITY and we DELIGHT in the DEATH of our DECEPTIVE DOING and DISORDERLY DEVICES. We're DRAWN away from DRAMA, DISCORD, and DISAPPOINTMENT, we DINE and DRINK with DAILY DEDICATION, and DESTRUCT, DESTROY, and DECAPITATE the DELUSIONS that DEMORALIZES our DETAILED DEVELOPMENT with DILIGENT DYNAMITE. Be the DIAMOND in our DIALOGUE as we DOCK in your DISTINGUISHED DOMINION and DOSE off and DRIFT into the DREAMS of our spiritual DUTIES. We now DIGRESS to DELIBERATE…And it is so!

BAILEY-OLOGY BLESSING:

Now Father, I seal this prophetic prayer of power in the Blood of Jesus and in the fresh wind of the Holy Spirit. I speak peace and power over every reader and those they will share this book with. Pour more into their Ministries, marriages, and money, then restore the joy of their salvation in you. Grant them clarity in their concerns, peace in the midst of their problems and joy in the midst of junk. Bring order into their lives and favor into their homes right now. AND IT IS SO in the mighty, majestic and marvelous name of Jesus, our Lord and Savior, we shout, pray, and celebrate. AMEN!

"The (E) Prayer of Power"

2 Corinthians 4:17, 18 - "For our light affliction, which is but for a moment, worketh for us a far more EXCEEDING and ETERNAL weight of glory; While we look not at the things which are seen, but at the things which are not seen: for the things which are seen are temporal; but the things which are not seen are ETERNAL."

ETERNAL Savior and Lord, how ENCOURAGED and EXCITED we are to ENTICE and EXPERIENCE an EXPLOSION of your EXTREME EXCELLENCE. Please ENDURE our EFFORTS to EXPRESS our EXALTATION despite the ENEMY'S EPIDEMIC to EXPOSE, EXPLOIT and ERASE us from EXISTING. EVERYBODY'S EXPECTATION to EXTOL you EARLY EVERYDAY will be ESTABLISHED and EXEMPLIFIED to the END of this ERA. We EXCLUSIVELY EVALUATE our ENVIRONMENT and we use our EARTHLY EQUIPMENT to EXTOL you. We are EASILY EAGER to EARN ELABORATE ELEVATION as we ELIMINATE EVERY ERRATIC ERUPTION of ERROR. We are ESPECIALLY ENTHUSIASTIC about the EXPENSIVE, yet EXCEEDING Blessing you've EXTENDED to the ENTIRE world. We don't want another EVENT or ENTERTAINMENT ENSEMBLE, but we ENTREAT the ENTRANCE of an ENCOUNTER to EMPOWER us and ERASE the ENTWINE of ENVY, ENRAGE, and ENDANGER. We come EMPTY and ENDEAVOR to ELECTRIFY,

EMPHASIZE and ENFORCE ENDURANCE as we EMBRACE and EAT the ELEMENTS of ETERNAL EQUALITY...And it is so!

BAILEY-OLOGY BLESSING:

Now Father, I seal this prophetic prayer of power in the Blood of Jesus and in the fresh wind of the Holy Spirit. I declare that every miracle, breakthrough, deliverance, way made, or open door be made manifest IMMEDIATELY for the purpose of producing power in your people. I speak fruitfulness into every reader and those they share this prayer with. We rest and relax in the peace of God now over every request. AND IT IS SO in the mighty, majestic and marvelous name of Jesus, our Lord and Savior, we shout, pray, and celebrate. AMEN!

"The (F) Prayer of Power"

> Proverbs 3:4 - "So shalt thou FIND FAVOUR and good understanding in the sight of God and man."

FIRST and FAR most, we the FEW, are FINE with the FRUITFUL FRANCHISE of your FIELD that FERTILIZES your FRESH FIRE. We thank you FATHER FOR FAITHFULLY FREEING us FROM the FATAL FIASCO of our FOES, FOR FUELING our FORTITUDE, FILLING our FACES with FOCUS, and FOR FORGIVING all our FAULTS, FILTH, and FAILURES. We will never FAIL to FORGET the FANTASTIC FAVOR you keep FREQUENTLY FORWARDING to FALL on all of us as we FEEN FOR more FOOD of the spiritual FLIGHT. We've FIGURED out how to FASHION our FEELINGS to FIT your FABULOUS FACADE as we FESTIVELY FAMILIARIZE ourselves with your FLEXIBLE and FIERY work. We don't FREAK out when that FOUL FOX try to FOOL the FATE of your FLEET, but we become FUGITIVES FOILING the FOLLY and FRICTION of the FRAUD. We bless you FOR the spiritual FILTER that FIXES the FAKENESS around us, FLINGS the FELONIES of the FALSELY accused, that FLUSHES FAMINES and the FATIGUE of our FAMILIES and FRIENDS. FINALLY, we FERVENTLY request your FINGER of love to FREEZE, FORCE and bring FORTH FORTUNES that will FINANCE the FAST FLOW of FUNDS FOREVER as we FINISH FIRMLY in FAITH and FOLLOW your FOOTSTEPS to FREEDOM…And it is so!

BAILEY-OLOGY BLESSING:

Now Father, I seal this prophetic prayer of power in the Blood of Jesus and in the fresh wind of the Holy Spirit. I declare fruitfulness into it and production out of it. I command your anointing to rest, rule and reign over every reader and the person they will share this prayer with. I decree and declare the dispatch of every angelic authority to minister into the lives of your people even NOW. AND IT IS SO in the mighty, majestic and marvelous name of Jesus, our Lord and Savior, we shout, pray, and celebrate. AMEN!

"The (G) Prayer of Power"

> Lamentations 3:22, 23 - "It is of the Lord's mercies that we are not consumed, because his compassions fail not. They are new every morning: GREAT is thy faithfulness."

GREAT GOD, we are so GRATEFUL that you've GENEROUSLY GRANTED us GRATUITOUS GIFTS and that the GATES of GLORY have GRABBED and GOVERNED our GAIN. We GLADLY GLOW in your GRACE and GIVE the GROTESQUE GIANTS that GAZE, GRAZE, and GROVEL at our GLOOM, a GOOD ole GASH and GLIMPSE of the GRAVE in the GROUND. Lord, please GUIDE our GREATNESS, GAUGE our GOINGS, and GET into our GESTURES as we GRASP and GATHER the GIGANTIC GEMS of spiritual GOLD. We expect a GRAND GUST of GUIDANCE to GRAVITATE and GUARD our hearts and minds as we GOUGE the GREED, GRIEF, GLUTTONY, and GRIP of the GRUESOME and GOTHIC GUERILLA. We GROIN, GRIND, and GLUE ourselves in the GREEN GRASS that GLORIFIES your GRANDEUR as you GRANT us GAS to GET pass GLOATING and GIMMICKS. We GENERALLY GERMINATE in GENETIC GLADNESS as the GET-A-LONG GANG stands in the GAP for GLOBAL GROWTH...And it is so!

BAILEY-OLOGY BLESSING:

Now Father, I seal this prophetic prayer of power in the Blood of Jesus and in the fresh wind of the Holy Spirit. I declare that the reader finds sweet serenity in this prayer as you unveil and uncover your unlimited blessings in their lives. I speak production, manifestation, increase and overflow over them and everything connected to them. I thank you for the release of them NOW. AND IT IS SO in the mighty, majestic and marvelous name of Jesus, our Lord and Savior, we shout, pray, and celebrate. AMEN!

"The (H) Prayer of Power"

2 Chronicles 7:14 - "If my people, which are called by my name, shall HUMBLE themselves, and pray, and seek my face, and turn from their wicked ways; then will I HEAR from HEAVEN, and will forgive their sin, and will HEAL their land."

*H*ELLO HOSPITABLE HOST, HERE your HEIRS are HANGING on the HINGES of HEARING from your HEART and as we HAVE our HOPE HEADING us towards a HARMONIOUS HARVEST. We make HASTE to HOLD on to the HELM of HOLINESS and we don't HESITATE to pay HOMAGE and shout HOSANNA to your HOVERING HAND. Continue to HIDE us from the HINDRANCE of HELL and HADES and from the HUMILIATION of the HITMAN as the HARMONY of HUMILITY HEAVE us into HONORING your name. We speak HIGH of HEAVEN, HOLLA out into the HEREAFTER with our HUMAN HORNS, and we HUNKER ourselves down at your HEEL. We HACK into HAPPINESS, put a HALT to all HOMICIDAL HORROR and HANDLE all HAVOC by canceling every HEX, HAUNTING HEATHEN, and HALLUCINATION sent to HIJACK our spiritual HOUSES. We HAVEN'T forgotten HOW to HANDLE our HATERS, HOWEVER, we make a HABIT out of HOPPING back to the HOOD to HOOKUP with those who need HELP and who desire to release HEAVINESS. We wear the HEADBAND, HALO, and HAT of HOLY HABITATION and HYDRATE ourselves with your living H20. We expect a HUMOROUS HANGOVER in HIM, HOLLERING

HALLELUJAH all down the HALLS of our HOMES. We HIKE towards your HEALING, HOISTING ourselves into HIBERNATION as we HYPE up the HYMNS from the HISTORY of HIS HALLOWED HERITAGE. Jesus, you are my HERO…And it is so!

BAILEY-OLOGY BLESSING:

Now Father, I seal this prophetic prayer of power in the Blood of Jesus and in the fresh wind of the Holy Spirit. I seek your guidance, provision, and prosperity to reign, rule and reside over each and every reader and those who they share this prayer with. I declare the release of your fire, fruitfulness, and fragrance to fall into the lives of your people as you revive, restore, and refresh us in your love. Manifest it all NOW. AND IT IS SO in the mighty, majestic and marvelous name of Jesus, our Lord and Savior, we shout, pray, and celebrate. AMEN!

"The (I) Prayer of Power"

Psalms 141:4 - "INCLINE not my heart to any evil thing, to practise wicked works with men that work iniquity: and let me not eat of their dainties."

*I*NFINITE God, we INQUIRE your INVESTMENT IN the IMPARTATION of your IMMEDIATE INSPIRATION. Please INSTRUCT us how to INCREASE the IMPACT of INDIVIDUAL INDEPENDENCE as you INTERVENE INSTANTLY IN our IMPURITIES, INSECURITIES, and IMPERFECTIONS. We are INCLINED to INVOLVE you IN the INSTRUMENTATION of your IMAGE as you make us IMMUNE to the IGNORANCE of all IMPOSTERS and INTRUDERS. We scratch the ITCH of IMPROVEMENT, IMPLEMENT soul INSPECTIONS, and ITEMIZE our IDEAS with the IMPRINT of your INTELLIGENCE. We know that IT'S of IMPERVIOUS IMPORTANCE that we IDENTIFY the INSANE ILLUSIONS of that ILLITERATE IDIOT who has IRRITATED our spiritual IMPULSES and IMITATED you whom he IDOLIZES. IT'S IN that INABILITY that we INCINERATE the ISSUES that INAPPROPRIATELY INCONVENIENCE us. We IMMENSELY IMMERSE ourselves IN the INHERITANCE of INCREASE and are IGNITED and IMPRESSED by your IMMACULATE ILLUSTRATIONS of INFALLIBLE love. Sometimes we feel INADEQUATE and INEFFECTIVE, but INDISCREETLY you keep INSERTING INFECTIOUS INFLUENCE IN our lives. INHABIT the INSIDES of our INNOCENCE and let your INCREDIBLE INSIGHT be

INSTALLED. We INSIST that you INTERRUPT our INTENTIONS as we INTIMATELY INTERJECT your IMMORTALITY INWARDLY. With INTENSIFIED INTELLECT, we don't sit in IDLED ISOLATED INCIDENTS, but declare that nothing IS IMPOSSIBLE for you. For you are our great INTERCESSOR…And it is so!

BAILEY-OLOGY BLESSING:

Now Father, I seal this prophetic prayer of power in the Blood of Jesus and in the fresh wind of the Holy Spirit. I speak wisdom, knowledge and understanding into every reader and those they are connected to share this prayer with. I RESPOND IMMEDIATELY to your text message and voicemail expecting something life-changing encounters to be imparted into your people, and from the sound of your voice, I anxiously await to see the manifestations released. IT IS SO!" in the mighty, majestic and marvelous name of Jesus, our Lord and Savior, we shout, pray, and celebrate. AMEN!

"The (J) Prayer of Power"

Hebrews 13:8 - "JESUS Christ the same yesterday, and today, and forever."

*J*EHOVAH JIREH, we are JUBILANT to JAR open up the JOURNAL of JUSTIFICATION and are JUMPY like JUNKIES with JOY at the name JESUS. We are JAUNTY in being a JUROR in the JAILING of the JOKER as we JOG out of the JAILHOUSE of JUSTICE. We wear the JEANS, JERSEYS, and JACKETS of the new JERUSALEM and denounce the JEWELRY of JUDGMENT. Please, JOIN the JAMBOREE of the JUST and JUDGE the JOKES of the JESTER, the JUNKYARD of the JEALOUS and the JURASSIC JUMBO of JEZEBEL. We remain JUICED, JOLLY and JITTERY in the JOURNEY understanding that the JINX, JEER, and JIGSAW of that devilish JUVENILE will receive a JOLT from our spiritual JAVELINS. We, your JEWELS, sing JINGLES of JAZZ as we JAB and JAM the JAW of the JACKAL which will JUMBLE the JET stream of that JIVE JERK. We spiritually JIG in your Heavenly JACKPOT, JIBE in the JACUZZI of our Kingdom JOBS, and are JOCUND in the JUNGLE like JOB. Move in a JIFFY as our JOINTS JAYWALK to the JOYFUL place of the JORDAN…And it is so!

BAILEY-OLOGY BLESSING:

Now Father, I seal this prophetic prayer of power in the Blood of Jesus and in the fresh wind of the Holy Spirit. I speak the release of your Super on our Natural as you fill our hearts with the anticipation of divine manifestation. I ask that you would release your favor and fruitfulness on and over everyone who reads this book and those who they will share it with. Be blessed in our efforts to bless you. "IT IS SO!" in the mighty, majestic and marvelous name of Jesus, our Lord and Savior, we shout, pray, and celebrate. AMEN!

"The (K) Prayer of Power"

Isaiah 26:3 - "Thou wilt KEEP him in perfect peace, whose mind is stayed on thee: because he trusteth in thee."

KIND KING, we KNEEL before you KNOWING that the KEYS to the KINGDOM lie in our KINSHIP with you. We KEEP KEEN sight on you, our KEEPER, who allows the KID in us to KILL the KIDNAPPER, KICKING him with KNOWLEDGE. We KARATE chop the KARMA of KOOKY KIBOSH, KNOCK-OFF the KNEES of the KILLER, and KINDLE the KISS of the all-knowing KNIGHT who KNOCKS on the doors of our hearts and KNEADS our lives. We also give you KUDOS for being the KEYNOTE speaker in our KINDNESS towards one another. We play KEYBOARDS and KAZOOS for you as we destroy the KNUCKLES and KNIVES of that KNAVISH KNACK. Thank you for KEEPING the hellhounds in their KENNEL and the enemy from going KAMIKAZE in our lives sending us to hell in KEROSENE soaked sins. You've KNITTED us together when we were out of KILTER, KEPT us together on an even KEEL, and tied a KNOT in our KINETIC ENERGY as we shout KAPUT to every KINK in the enemy's KIT. For you are our KEYSTONE…And it is so!

BAILEY-OLOGY BLESSING:

Now Father, I seal this prophetic prayer of power in the Blood of Jesus and in the fresh wind of the Holy Spirit. I speak the release of joy, peace, and prosperity over, around, and on every person who reads this book and for those they will share it with. Bless their mindsets, their Ministries, their marriages/relationships, and their money abundantly. I speak INCREASE, ABUNDANCE, and OVERFLOW into their lives this day. "IT IS SO!" in the mighty, majestic and marvelous name of Jesus, our Lord and Savior, we shout, pray, and celebrate. AMEN!

"The (L) Prayer of Power"

1 John 4:7, 8 - "Beloved, let us LOVE one another: for LOVE is of God; and everyone that LOVETH is born of God, and knoweth God. He that LOVETH not knoweth not God; for God is LOVE."

LILLY of the Valley, please LAND and LINGER in the LABORATORIES of our LIVES as we LACE our LIPS with a LITANY of scriptures. We LIVE in the LOVE of you, our LORD and LONG to LIFT the LEVELS of each LAYMAN as we LEAN on the LEGACY of the LIVING LIGHT. Your word is never LIBEL nor LIES, but gives us LEVERAGE to LACERATE the LIMBS of the LEWD LEACH'S. LEND us the LICENSE to LEAP on the LIEUTENANT of the LEGIONS, LEAVE behind LAZINESS, and LIBERATE the LOST as we LINK ourselves to the LEGITIMATE LINEAGE of the LAMB. We LAUNCH ourselves away from the LIAR who LURES us into a LUSTFUL and LASCIVIOUS LIFESTYLE LEADING us to LOUNGE with a LACKADAISICAL attitude in our LOYALTY and LABOR for Christ. We LASER and LEVEL the LODGE of that LOUSY, LOWDOWN LEPER, not with LIMP, LIBRARY LINGO, but as a LINGUIST with LOUD LANGUAGE. We declare that we're not LAME, LOOPY, nor LONELY in this LAND, but LUMINESCENT LOOSED LONGEVITY. You are LITERALLY the LEADER of a Holy LEAGUE of LIMITLESS believers. So, restore back the years of our LUCRATIVE LOT we LACKED as we LEAVE the LOCUST and LEVIATHAN in a LETHAL LULLABY. We speak no LACK, LIMITATION, nor LAMENTATION in our LIVES, but LEGALIZE LAVISH LIFE in a LARGE way…And it is so!

BAILEY-OLOGY BLESSING:

Now Father, I seal this prophetic prayer of power in the Blood of Jesus and in the fresh wind of the Holy Spirit. I speak life and longevity over every person who will read this book and for those they will share it with. I command an extraordinary move of your Spirit to be released on their behalf today as you get the Glory out of their worship, work, and witness. Be ABUNDANTLY BLESSED, Oh God, in our attempt to give you the best we have. "IT IS SO!" in the mighty, majestic and marvelous name of Jesus, our Lord and Savior, we shout, pray, and celebrate. AMEN!

"The (M) Prayer of Power"

Psalms 34:3 - "O MAGNIFY the Lord with me, and let us exalt his name together."

MOST Holy MESSIAH, thanks for MAXIMIZING the MANIFESTATIONS of MIRACLES over MY life. You have MADE ME MERCIFUL even in the MIDST of MY MANISH MISTAKES, MISCHIEVOUS MISHAPS, and MAJOR MANIPULATIONS and MALFUNCTIONS. MAKE every MALICIOUS MONSTER and MASQUERADE MORON MELTDOWN and MANEUVER MOTIONLESS under your MIGHTY, MAJESTIC hand. We MOLD and MENTOR the MENTALITIES of MANY MULTITUDES MATURLY, as the MANNA of your MOVEMENT remains MATCHLESS. So, keep MOTIVATING the MINDS, MINISTRIES, and MARRIAGES of MANKIND and MIRACULOUSLY MOVE MOUNTAINS as we MINISTER to the MASSES. MEET us in every MISSION, MODIFY our MEAGER METHODS, and MULTIPLY the MAGNITUDE of MERITS. MEND our broken hearts from the MOLESTATION of that MENACING MANIAC. We MELODIOUSLY MAGNIFY you, dear MASTER in MEEKNESS as we MANAGE to MEET you in a MOBILE MERGER. MAY a MEMORABLE METAMORPHOSIS take place MAINLY from our MOUTHS to produce MUCH MORE in our lives..And it is so!

BAILEY-OLOGY BLESSING:

Now Father, I seal this prophetic prayer of power in the Blood of Jesus and in the fresh wind of the Holy Spirit. I speak favor and fruitfulness over this Word. Manifest it immediately for every person who reads this book and everyone they will share it with. Release your Glory upon them and everything that concerns them NOW. "IT IS SO!" in the mighty, majestic and marvelous name of Jesus, our Lord and Savior, we shout, pray, and celebrate. AMEN!

"The (N) Prayer of Power"

Hebrews 11:1 - "NOW faith is the substance of things hoped for, the evidence of things not seen."

Jehovah NISSI, we NOMINATE you to NAVIGATE the NATURE of our NATION. Please NARRATE the NOVELS of the NOBLE and NOTARIZE a NEW NONSTOP NOURISHMENT over the NOVICE. We give NOTICE to NEGATIVITY and to the NOISE of the NIGHT CRAWLER, that at the NAME of the NAZARITE, who is NEAR, the NORMAL NUDGING, NAGGING and NERVE-RACKING NUISANCES will be NULL and NO more. We leave NO room for NAYSAYERS who NEGATE our promises and NEUTER the NEWNESS of productivity. Give us the NECESSARY NOBILITY to be NICE to our NEIGHBORS and to NURTURE the NETWORK of the NEGLECTED. We declare that NOW is the time to NEUTRALIZE every NUT with NOTHING to do and NOWHERE to go. And although we are NAUGHTY by NATURE, we ask that you would guide us through the NARROW paths as we NATURALLY lift your NAME. We thank you from the NATIVITY to the NAILS. NEVER again will we be NAIVE to the NERVE of our NEMESIS, but we spread the NEWS that you are NIGH and we NEED you. NONE will be NON-RESPONSIVE to your NEXT blessing because you've NOTARIZED a NUMERICAL NUCLEUS...And it is so!

BAILEY-OLOGY BLESSING:

Now Father, I seal this prophetic prayer of power in the Blood of Jesus and in the fresh wind of the Holy Spirit. I speak next dimension prosperity and blessing over your people and everything connected to them. I declare that your promises are definite and your peace is delivered to each of them who reads this book and those they will share it with. Be totally blessed by our efforts to bring glory to your name and power into our purpose. "IT IS SO!" in the mighty, majestic and marvelous name of Jesus, our Lord and Savior, we shout, pray, and celebrate. AMEN!

"The (O) Prayer of Power"

1 John 4:4 - "Ye are of God, little children, and have OVERCOME them: because greater is he that is in you than he that is in the world."

OH God, OUR OMEGA, we OPENINGLY OFFER OURSELVES to be ORCHESTRATED by the OATH of ORDER as we OVERDOSE ON OBEDIENCE and OBSCURE from OUTRAGEOUS OPPONENTS who cause us to OMIT OUR OBLIGATIONS as OVERCOMERS. Please OVERSEE the OBSTRUCTION OF any and all OBSTACLES OF OPPRESSION and OPPOSITION as we OCCUPY every OPPORTUNITY for OURSELVES to OBTAIN the OIL OF spiritual OPERATION. We OFFICIALLY OBEY you, OUR OWNER even when we're the OSTRACIZED OUTCAST and when OUTSTANDING ODDS are OFTEN OMINOUS. We are OPTIMISTIC that OUR ORDAINED praise will OBLITERATE the OFFENSIVE ODOR OF sin and we take OUR OUTREACH to another OCTAVE. We speak the OUTPOUR OF an OVERAGE OF OPULENCE ON and in OUR lives as we OBSERVE your OMNIPOTENT, OMNISCIENT, OMNI-PRESENT and OMNI-DIRECTIONAL name. We cut OUT the OPINIONS OF OPPORTUNISTS that OPEN up ORTHODOX debates and we're OBLIGED to OVERTAKE and OVERPOWER the OVERWHELMING madness OF OTHERS. We're OKAY in this ONGOING walk, because you're the ONLY OMNISCIENT God we OUGHT to be OFFERING OUR ORGANISMS to. So, we shout with OOMPH to the ONE, true and ORIGINAL God..And it is so!

BAILEY-OLOGY BLESSING:

Now Father, I seal this prophetic prayer of power in the Blood of Jesus and in the fresh wind of the Holy Spirit. I speak your Glory on it and over it as we collectively speak it by faith. I declare your supernatural manifestation to overtake and overpower every person who reads this book as well as to those they will share it with. Reveal yourself to us NOW and release into us your favor, fire, and fruitfulness. Be extremely gratified with our efforts to bring your name honor and Glory. "IT IS SO!" in the mighty, majestic and marvelous name of Jesus, our Lord and Savior, we shout, pray, and celebrate. AMEN!

"The (P) Prayer of Power"

Colossians 3:15 - "And let the PEACE of God rule in your hearts, to which also ye are called in one body; and be ye thankful."

Awesome PRINCE of PEACE, let the POWER of your PROVISION, PASS through our PRE-DESTINED PLACES and PULL us out of every PURPOSELESS PLAN and PITIFUL PROCRASTINATION we've PUT ourselves in. We PAUSE in our PASSIONATE PRESSING to PETITION for your PERDURABLE PROTECTION and are PRIVILEGED and POSITIONED to PARTAKE in the PRIZE of PRAISE and PRECIPITOUS of spiritual PROCLIVITY, as we PREPARE to PARLAY with the most POWERFUL PHENOMENON to ever PART the PLANET. PHASE out every PREPOSTEROUS, PENALTY, and PRINCIPALITY that attempts to PUSH us into spiritual PRISON. We do not PROFESS to be PERFECT, but we PRACTICE daily, to PROMOTE your love and PERSUADE your PEOPLE to be more PERSONABLE with you. Don't be PERTURBED by our PETTINESS, but PERUSE the PERIMETERS of our PHYSICALITY and become our PHYSICIAN who PENETRATES and PICKLOCKS every PIECE of our PRECIOUS and PRICELESS PILGRIMAGE. We PARADE as PIONEERS of PIETY and cancel the PLAGUES of PODIUM PIMPS who POISON each PERSON with POETIC and PROPHETIC POO-POO. We cancel every PROBLEM, PAIN, and PROHIBITION that is PROPOSED by the PROSECUTOR of that PERSECUTOR and PROTEST PHYSICAL and PSYCHOLOGICAL PUBLICATIONS.

Lord, PLEASE keep us POSITIONED to PORTRAY you POSITIVELY and release a PLETHORA of POTENT PRESBYTERY who will POUR out PRAYERS that will PRECISELY PROVOKE your PROMISES. We will remain POISED in our PURPOSE and PUMPED up in our POTENTIAL as we POINT the PARISHIONERS to the PERILOUS PERIOD PRICE, you PAID that was PASSED to you to make us PARTAKERS of your PLENTEOUS PAVILION. We are PREGNANT with POSSIBILITIES and will continue to keep PRESSING to the PRESENCE of the POTTER…And it is so!

BAILEY-OLOGY BLESSING:

Now Father, I seal this prophetic prayer of power in the Blood of Jesus and in the fresh wind of the Holy Spirit. I speak that your promises concerning the life of the person or people reading this prayer be made manifest before their very eyes. I speak and seek the release of your Glory to rest, rule, and reign on, over, around, and in them from now to forever and that they will be empowered and endowed by the movement of your Holy Spirit. Lord God, fill them to the brim with all supernatural blessings, favor, and be gratified and satisfied with our attempts to keep you first in our lives. "IT IS SO!" in the mighty, majestic and marvelous name of Jesus, our Lord and Savior, we shout, pray, and celebrate. AMEN!

"The (Q) Prayer of Power"

Hebrews 4:12 - "For the word of God is QUICK, and powerful, and sharper than any two-edged sword, piercing even to the dividing asunder of soul and spirit, and of the joints and marrow, and is a discerner of the thoughts and intents of the heart."

QUINTESSENTIAL Lord, please QUADRUPLE, even QUINTUPLE, the QUALITY of our QUARTERS and QUANTUM leap us out of the QUICKSAND as we QUARANTINE the QUARRELS of the QUACKS and QUENCH the QUITTING of the QUAINT. Let our QUEENS to be QUILTED and QUITE satisfied with love without having to QUAKE, QUIVER, or have QUESTIONS. Lead the QUORUM of the QUALIFIED in soul-saving QUOTAS while QUICKLY QUEUEING the QUALMS of the QUIRKY. Thank you Lord for QUIDDITY, for giving us QUIETUDE, and for allowing us to be QUIP. Please QUIET the QUIBBLES of our QUEST and QUOTIENT every QUIZ we face in life…And it is so!

BAILEY-OLOGY BLESSING:

Now Father, I seal this prophetic prayer of power in the Blood of Jesus and in the fresh wind of the Holy Spirit. I speak that your blood covers the content of this prayer and that you would reveal your work to the reader even now. Unveil and Unleash peace, power, and prosperity on the place that they are currently in and make yourself clear enough for them to understand your Will, Word, and ways. Have your way even now. I bind every demon and devil sent to distract or disrupt this prayer from being answered. You get all of the Glory, honor, and praise "IT IS SO!" in the mighty, majestic and marvelous name of Jesus, our Lord and Savior, we shout, pray, and celebrate. AMEN!

"The (R) Prayer of Power"

Philippians 4:4 – "REJOICE in the Lord always: and again I say, REJOICE."

Jehovah RAPHA, as we RIDE the ROLLERCOASTER and ROAM the ROUGH RIDGES of life, we RUN with REVERENCE towards your presence and we're RADICALLY READY to RECEIVE the REWARDS and RICHES that we are RECORDED to REAP and RECOVER. We REPENT and RESPECTFULLY REQUEST REAL RESTORATION to REST on and REVIVE the REJOICING of those who've been RATTLED, RUFFED UP and RUINED by the ROARING RAGE of that RASCAL of REBELLION and RESTRICTION. We REQUIRE to be REBUILT, REMASTERED, REPLENISHED and RECONSTRUCTED in RIGHTEOUSNESS through the REDEMPTION of your RIGHT hand. We REMEMBER not to allow RITUALS and ROUTINES of life to RESTRICT our RELATIONSHIP with you. We RECOGNIZE that we need you daily to REARRANGE and RECALIBRATE our minds and then REMOVE any RIDICULOUS RUSES and RESENTMENTS in our hearts. We will not RETREAT nor RETRACT from our kingdom RESPONSIBILITIES, but we will continue to RECALL, RELY ON, and RESEARCH your Word so we can REPRESENT you RIGHT. Holy REDEEMER, please RESET and REIGNITE your fire in us and REMIND us that you never work in REWIND, but allow REDUCTION to REALIGN us. Continue to REVEAL who you are to us and REVERT our minds, hearts, and spirits back to your RESUME of the ROWS of ROOMS you keep making for us to be ultimately RAPTURED and not RUPTURED. We will be REMISS if we don't RESPOND with a RAVE of REWARDING REPORTS about how you REPAID that ROGUE for trying to RETALIATE on the RIGHTEOUS. Lord, you allowed us to RETURN back to you, you've RELEASED us from REPLYING our past, and you REFUSE to watch us RELIVE what you've REMOVED out of our lives. Thanks for RESURRECTING, REPAIRING and REPOSITIONING our minds, bodies, and spirits and REASSEMBLING and REASSIGNING us back to the place you originally wanted us to be…And it is so!

BAILEY-OLOGY BLESSING:

Now Father, I seal this prophetic prayer of power in the Blood of Jesus and in the fresh wind of the Holy Spirit. I speak that the reader finds you moving in the midst of their lives and that every miracle, blessing and breakthrough comes expeditiously with no delay and no denial. Let your power prevail and your peace penetrate every place that they are currently in. Show us your Glory and continue to reveal your majesty to us. "IT IS SO!" in the mighty, majestic and marvelous name of Jesus, our Lord and Savior, we shout, pray, and celebrate. AMEN!

"The (S) Prayer of Power"

James 1:19 – "Wherefore, my beloved brethren, let every man be SWIFT to hear, SLOW to SPEAK, SLOW to wrath."

SOVEREIGN SAVIOR, as we SCREEN and SURVEY our SURROUNDINGS, we SEEK your STRENGTH to SATURATE our SPIRITS with SOUNDNESS and STABILITY in the midst of SITUATIONS, SELF STRUGGLES and STAGNATION. We SEARCH for your SHEKINAH Glory to SCRAPE us out of and SEAL us from the SEDUCTIONS, SICKNESSES, and STUPIDITY that will keep us STUCK in SCATTERED SCENARIOS. We ask that you SHRED the SCHISMS that would SEPARATE us from having a SEAT by your SIDE. We SALUTE you for STRATEGICALLY SAVING the SOULS of every SINNER, for SHEPHERDING the SERVICE of the SAINTS, and for SWIFTLY STOPPING the SHENANIGANS of that SCANDALOUS SCOUNDREL. We SUGGEST and SUBMIT that you would SHOCK the STINGS of that SNEAKY SERPENT, STRIP us of the SCUM SCHEDULED as a SET up by the SCHEMING of SATAN, and SHATTER the SCOOP SENT to SABOTAGE and make a SPECTACLE out of our SACRIFICE. Let our SHOUTS of SPIRITUAL SPEECH SHIFT and SHAKE up our SHELTERS and SYNAGOGUES and let our SCENERIES be STABILIZED with the SCENT of SERENITY and the SWEET SMELLING SAVOR of your STOREHOUSE. Now Oh Lord, SUPPLY SUPPORT to those who are SIMPLY SURVIVING, SCOUT out and STIR up SOME STUFF in us SO we can SPEAK as STRONG

SOLDIERS, and SUPERVISE, SUPERINTEND, and SECURE our SOCIETY and the SECTIONS we STAY in by SENDING the angels to SAVE us from the STRAIN of not having SUBSTANCE. We SIT in the SECRET place of the SUPERNATURAL and we're SUBMISSIVE and SATISFIED in your SUPREME SWAG..And it is so!

BAILEY-OLOGY BLESSING:

Now Father, I seal this prophetic prayer of power in the Blood of Jesus and in the fresh wind of the Holy Spirit. I speak that the request is supplied and the requester is satisfied with the outcome. We thank you for allowing the release of every blessing, miracle, and manifestation to make its arrival and we glorify you that every word spoken will not return void back to you. Let nothing be done or said in vain glory, but for you to get all of the Glory, honor, and praise for all we are and what we will be. "IT IS SO!" in the mighty, majestic and marvelous name of Jesus, our Lord and Savior, we shout, pray, and celebrate. AMEN!

The (T) Prayer of Power

Psalms 37:3 – "TRUST in the LORD, and do good; so shalt thou dwell in the land, and verily thou shalt be fed."

Holy TUTELARY, TODAY we TESTIFY THAT you're TRUE, TENDER, and TANGIBLE, we TOTALLY TRUST THAT you're TAKING us THROUGH TIMES of TRIALS and TESTS TO TRAIN and TEACH us THE TREASURES of being TRIUMPHANT. We THANK you for TAILORING a TABLE for us in, THE THICK of THE TAUNTS, TACTICS, and THREATS of THAT TERRIBLE TALEBEARER. We THRIVE TO TRASH THE THOUGHTS designed TO TAINT and TERRIFY us from TELEPORTING into the THRESHOLD of your TERRIFIC presence and we bless you for THE TOOLS and TECHNIQUES TRANSFERRED into us TO TACKLE and TO TEAR down THE THEATRICS, THEORY, and THEOLOGY of THAT THIRSTY THUG who continuously TRIES to TANGLE us in TEMPORARY TRIBULATION. We won't TOLERATE THE TABOO of being THE TAIL, so we use our TALENTS, TITHES, and TITLES to TERMINATE THE TEMPLES of THE TEMPTER, THE TRAPS of THE THIEF, and THE TORMENTS of THAT THREATENING TERRORIST. So, we TAG TEAM with THE TRINITY, THE TENDENCY TO TOUCH THE lives of THOSE who need a THERAPEUTIC TASTE of THE TERRITORY you've TIMELY prepared at THE TOP. Even THOUGH THE TRAIL TOWARDS THAT TOMORROW got TIGHT, TOUGH, and TEDIOUS, we can TALK about our TRANSFORMATION and TELL others THE

THINGS NEEDED TO TRANSITION and reach THE THRONE of Grace TOO. Lord, your TROOPS are THOROUGHLY TARRYING and THROWING away THE TIES THAT bind and TAMPER with us as we set THE TONE TO express TO THOSE TRAVELING with us THAT we are THINE'S…And it is so!

BAILEY-OLOGY BLESSING:

Now Father, I seal this prophetic prayer of power in the Blood of Jesus and in the fresh wind of the Holy Spirit. I speak that the loads on the lives of your people are lifted, the weights of worrying about things working out are cast away, and that your supernatural authority, majesty, and power prevails in all areas of our lives. Defend your place and peace in the lives of those who desire your presence and open us up for us to receive the manifold blessings and benefits you've promised. You get all of the Glory, honor, and praise "IT IS SO!" in the mighty, majestic and marvelous name of Jesus, our Lord and Savior, we shout, pray, and celebrate. AMEN!

"The (U) Prayer of Power"

2 Samuel 6:22a (NKJV) – "And I will be even more UNDIGNIFIED than this, and will be humble in my own sight."

Almighty UPLIFTER, we thank you for UNDERGIRDING US UNDER the UMBRELLA of your ULTIMATE power and wisdom. UNDOUBTEDLY, you have UPLOADED an UNLIMITED supply of UNIQUENESS in US and with UNDERSTANDING of who you've created, you've UNCONVENTIONALLY and UNCONDITIONALLY held US UP UNDER your mighty hand. Thank you for UNCOVERING our gifts, UTILIZING our skills and abilities, and UNLEASHING UNEXPECTED, UNEXPLAINED blessings to US. Lord, we can remain UNITED and UNATTACHED from UNFRUITFUL and UNEQUALLY yoked people. Please UNARM any UNACCEPTABLE, UGLIFIED behavior that UPSETS you and remove any UNAUTHORIZED UPROARS that breeds UNBELIEF. We were UNAWARE that your UBIQUITY is UNCHARTED and UNCHANGING, yet we USHER in the USAGE of your UNDIGNIFIED UPGRADES as we URGE with URGENCY for you to UPROOT and UNDO any UNORGANIZED, UNKIND and UNSTABLE thing in US. Lord, please UPRISE and UNBIND us from UNFORTUNATE pains and UPDATE our UNTOUCHED and UNTOLD assignments in the UNIVERSE. Please UNWRAP and UNMASK the UTTERANCES from UPSTAIRS UNTIL you UNVEIL the UNKNOWN for US to USE for the Kingdom. UNLOCK the UNDENIABLE, UNBURDEN the UNBALANCED, and make UNITS out of the USELESS…And it is so!

BAILEY-OLOGY BLESSING:

Now Father, I seal this prophetic prayer of power in the Blood of Jesus and in the fresh wind of the Holy Spirit. I speak that every word spoken throughout this book has ministered and moved on the hearts, minds, and spirits of your people. I decree and declare that your promises come quickly to each person with no delay and no denial as download your power, and peace while they wait. Get the Glory out of us all. "IT IS SO!" in the mighty, majestic and marvelous name of Jesus, our Lord and Savior, we shout, pray, and celebrate. AMEN!

"The (V) Prayer of Power"

1 Peter 5:8 – "Be sober, be VIGILANT; because your adversary the devil, as a roaring lion, walketh about, seeking whom he may devour."

Father, with VIGOR and VIGILANCE, we VIBRANTLY VOICE our VICTORIOUS VOCABULARY with VOLUME over the VARIOUS VENTURES you VIVIDLY allow us to VALLEY through. We cover ourselves in the VESTMENTS of VIRTUE in order to VACUUM and VACCINATE the VULGARITY of VENALITY and we VANQUISH to VAPOR the VAGUE and VAINGLORY place in the VEINS of our VOWS designed to VIOLATE the VISIONS you gave us and the VERSIONS you made us to be. We thank you for the VERACITY that gives us the VELOCITY to VINDICATE us from the VICES of the VULTURES and VILLAINS as we VERBALIZE VENGEANCE on the VENOM of the VICIOUS VIPER and the VANITY of the VANDALS. We VALIANTLY VACATE on the VERGE of VIEWING the VARIETIES of things you have VERSED and VOCALIZE for us to VISUALIZE in your Heavenly VAULTS. As VALETS and VOLUNTEERS of our VALIDATED VOCATIONS, we VERIFY that the VASTNESS of your VALUABLE VERSATILITY will never VANISH as the VEHICLE of your VISITATION VENTILATES and VERSIFIES every VICTIM into VICTORS and VISIONARIES...And it is so!

BAILEY-OLOGY BLESSING:

Now Father, I seal this prophetic prayer of power in the Blood of Jesus and in the fresh wind of the Holy Spirit. I speak that every believer reaches a place in you that will open up their hearts for you to open up Heaven to and for them. I ask that everything they need is met, every desire is fulfilled, and every request is granted the moment they believe and you will do it without delay. You will get all of the Glory and honor because it is due unto you. "IT IS SO!" in the mighty, majestic and marvelous name of Jesus, our Lord and Savior, we shout, pray, and celebrate. AMEN!

"The (W) Prayer of Power"

Romans 8:1 - "There is therefore now no condemnation to them which are in Christ Jesus, who WALK not after the flesh, but after the Spirit."

WISE and WONDERFUL One, WE WILLFULLY extend a WARM-HEARTED WELCOME to you as you WOW us WITH the WEALTH of your WORD and the WORKS of your WISDOM. We WADE in the WATERS of WORSHIP and WE WAIT in WONDER knowing that you WOULD make a WAY for us to WEATHER the WACKINESS of the WILDERNESS. WALK WITH us as WE WASTE no time WAGING WAR against the WICKEDNESS and WILES of the WITCHES and WARLOCKS sent to WEAKEN our moments and WOUND our minds in You. Our WAILING and WAVING WILL cancel out the WRONG and WE WEND and WHIRL to the WELLS WHERE you WANT us to drink from. WE also WRITE as a WEAPON to WRECK the WALLS of WANDERING, WRETCHEDNESS, and WORRY. WE WITHDRAW ourselves under the WATCHFUL eye of your mighty WIND. Now, WHISPER through the WINDOWS of your WILL to WAKE up our WORTH. WASH us WHITE, make us WHOLE and WIPE away all WEEPING and WORLDLY WOES WHILE WE WITNESS WITH other WORKERS as WINNERS and not WALLOPERS...And it is so!

BAILEY-OLOGY BLESSING:

Now Father, I seal this prophetic prayer of power in the Blood of Jesus and in the fresh wind of the Holy Spirit. I speak that every prophetic word uttered would be honored by your goodness and your Glory and that nothing would go lacking or lost in our lives. Continue to do and develop in us the tools and techniques for us to remain faithful and fruitful in life and remove any and all hindrances sent to determine us from that destined place. Father, you get the glory out of our lives."IT IS SO!" in the mighty, majestic and marvelous name of Jesus, our Lord and Savior, we shout, pray, and celebrate. AMEN!

"The (X) Prayer of Power"

Psalms 127:1 – "EXCEPT the LORD build the house, they labour in vain that build it: EXCEPT the LORD keep the city, the watchman waketh but in vain."

Lord, we make no XCUSE for being (X) XHIBITIONISTS, XTREMISTS and XCONS. However, we XPERIMENT with XCITEMENT XPOSING and XPLAINING the XTRAORDINARY XAMPLE you've XPRESSED. Please X-RAY our spiritual XYLOPHONES and XTRACT any XPOSURE to XCESSIVE behavior that will XILE our XUBERANCE. We XALT and XTOL you XPECTING to XPAND our XPERIENCE in your XISTENCE…And it is so!

BAILEY-OLOGY BLESSING:

Now Father, I seal this prophetic prayer of power in the Blood of Jesus and in the fresh wind of the Holy Spirit. I speak that the working power of the anointing destroys every work of darkness and every yolk that binds. We dispatch your angels to encamp around every believer and person who desires to believe beyond their current place and position. Free us with your blood and let your Glory provide and prevail. "IT IS SO!" in the mighty, majestic and marvelous name of Jesus, our Lord and Savior, we shout, pray, and celebrate. AMEN!

"The (Y) Prayer of Power"

James 3:17 – "But the wisdom that is from above is first pure, then peaceable, gentle, willing to YIELD, full of mercy and good fruits, without partiality and without hypocrisy."

YAHWEH, we dare not YAMMER or YELP today, because we said YES to YOU YESTERDAY, YET we still YARE to YANK on YOUR YOKE to prevent us from YAWING our YEAR. We YAWN at the YODEL of the enemy as YOU prove YOURSELF like only YOU can. We YEARN like YEOMEN at the YUMMINESS of YOUR Word and YELL, "YAHOO" and "YIPPEE" like YOUNGSTERS YELLING in the YARD. We YIELD to YOU up YONDER and we know YOU'LL be proud to call us YOURS… And it is so!

BAILEY-OLOGY BLESSING:

Now Father, I seal this prophetic prayer of power in the Blood of Jesus and in the fresh wind of the Holy Spirit. I speak that the fresh fire of the Holy One will rest on the hearts, minds, and souls of every believer now and that you would carry and catapult us into the dimension of blessings and favor. Have thine way in us, through us, and around us and get all of the Glory both now and forever. "IT IS SO!" in the mighty, majestic and marvelous name of Jesus, our Lord and Savior, we shout, pray, and celebrate. AMEN!

"The (Z) Prayer of Power"

Psalms 50:2 – "Out of ZION, the perfection of beauty, God hath shined."

Lord, even though we're at the last letter of the alphabe we take nothing from the impact of its punch. So Lord, we ZOOM and ZERO in on our ZEAL with ZEST for you to ZIGZAG through the ZOO of ZANINESS and ZAP the ZIP CODE of the ZOMBIES. Please ZONE the ZEPHYR of ZION and don't waste ZILCH on the ZING of our ZITHER…And it is so!

BAILEY-OLOGY BLESSING:
Now Father, I seal this prophetic prayer of power in the Blood of Jesus and in the fresh wind of the Holy Spirit. I speak that you Oh God will seal every prayer prayed with your blood, love, and promises. I ask that you would unleash and unveil the very thing that we need to keep pushing and being productive in the Kingdom. Do not delay in doing what you promised and continue to allow your Glory to rest, rule, and reside in us. "IT IS SO!" in the mighty, majestic and marvelous name of Jesus, our Lord, and Savior, we shout, pray, and celebrate. AMEN!

"The (A To Z) Prayer of Power"

Ephesians 4:6 - "One God and Father of ALL, who is above ALL, and through ALL, and in you ALL."

(A)LMIGHTY (B)LESSER, (C)ONTINUE (D)ELIVERING (E)VERYBODY (F)ROM (G)REED (H)INDERING (I)DEAS ... Lord (J)ESUS, (K)INDLY (L)ET (M)ERCY (N)OW (O)PEN (P)ROSPEROUS (Q)UESTS, (R)EVERSE (S)ATANIC (T)RAPS and (U)NVEIL (V)ICTORIOUS (W)ORKS (X)POSING (Y)OUR (Z)EAL... And it is so!

BAILEY-OLOGY BLESSING:

Now Father, I seal this prophetic prayer of power in the Blood of Jesus and in the fresh wind of the Holy Spirit. I speak your wonder-working power over the life of the person who reads this book and those who they'll share it with. I request and require a major move of manifestation to embrace and embalm the lives of your people as we endeavor to give you all the Glory, honor, and praise. Let your Spirit speak, your Anointing adjust, your Favor fall, and your Hand heal every believer's life. "IT IS SO!" in the mighty, majestic and marvelous name of Jesus, our Lord and Savior, we shout, pray, and celebrate. AMEN!

The Outroduction

The bible says in **Colossians 3:17 (KJV)**, *"And WHATSOEVER ye do IN WORD OR DEED, DO ALL in the name of the Lord Jesus, giving thanks to God and the Father by him."* Now that you've learned how to pray, How to prophetically stop the enemy from stopping your prayers, How to watch what you say and how you say it, and how to prophetically pray alphabetically into your life, you can now do effectively what God commands you to do in your purpose. Please remember, that every purpose has a promise and every promise produces purpose. So, the next time you want to know your purpose in this life, remember what the Word of God says in **1 Thessalonians 5:16-18 (KJV)**, *"Rejoice evermore. Pray without ceasing. IN EVERYTHING give thanks: for this is the will of God in Christ Jesus concerning you."* In other words, IN

DEBT
DISTRESS and
DIVORCE
PAIN
PERSECUTION and
PROBLEMS
SORROW
SADNESS and
STRUGGLES
HURT
HEARTACHE and
HEARTBREAK
TRIAL

TROUBLE and
TURMOIL
BITTERNESS
BATTEREDNESS and
BROKENNESS, God says, "**TO GIVE THANKS!**"

People of God, you have been divinely picked to fulfill the purpose of God in your life which means everything you go through and will endure is only a part of the production process of the promise. For the bible says in **James 1:1-4 (KJV)**, *"James, a servant* **(a person in the service of another)** *of God and of the Lord Jesus Christ, to the twelve tribes which are scattered abroad* **(sown throughout; purposely planted)**, *greeting. My brethren, count it all joy when ye fall into divers temptations; Knowing this, that the trying* **(testing the effect or result of)** *of your faith worketh patience* **(the ability to handle, endure, or suppress annoyances, misfortune, or pain without complaint)**. *But let patience have her perfect* **(complete)** *work, that ye may be perfect and entire* **(whole; full all the way through)**, *wanting nothing."* In other words, God purposely planted you in various situations and circumstances to test the effect and result of your faith. He does it so your faith can give birth to patience, which will complete the work in you, leaving you full and complete in Him. God's productive plan for your life is to bring you to a place of fruitfulness in Him.

Therefore, you cannot die until the work of your purpose is complete. Meaning, you've been given a divine purpose to fulfill while you are here on earth and prayer will empower you to accomplish that purpose in your life. When Jesus had accomplished His work down here on earth, He said in **John 19:30 (KJV)**, *"It is finished and then He gave up the ghost."* Paul said in **2 Timothy 4:6-8 (KJV)**, *"For I am now ready to be offered, and the time of my departure is at hand. I have fought a good fight, I have finished my course, and I have kept the faith: Henceforth there is laid up for* me a crown of righteousness, which the Lord, the righteous judge, shall give me at that day: and not to me only, but unto all them also that love his appearing." In other words, you've been sent here by God to accomplish a work and it will be fulfilled through you for the sake of the Kingdom.

As this book reaches its culmination, I shout with elation and elevation into your spirit, that you must seek, through prayer and praise, the real purpose of God for your life so that you will be complete and whole, wanting nothing. For the bible declares in **Philippians 2:5 (KJV)**, *"Let this mind be in you, which was also in Christ Jesus."* Meaning, if you keep your mind focused on the assignment set for your hands to complete, your purpose in its completion will bring prosperity into your life. For the bible says in **Matthew 6:33 (KJV) *my favorite passage***, *"But seek ye first the kingdom of God, and his righteousness; and all these things shall be added unto you."* You have been released in this hour with the power of the Most High God to carry out and fulfill every single promise designed for your life. Now is the time for the real believers, MEN and WOMEN, to stand up and "P"

PRAY (Seek Life)
PREACH (Share Life)
PRAISE (Shout Life)
PROPHESY (Speak Life)

For this is the Will of God concerning you and this will help your purpose be fulfilled. So, start prophetically praying over your life today so that the power of God can produce prosperity in your life!

The Gift For Your Support

Thank you so much for purchasing **HOW TO PROPHETICALLY PRAY OVER YOUR PURPOSE!** I pray that you were tremendously blessed by this book and moved to become a productive prophet over your own purpose. And to show my appreciation for your love and support of this book, I would like to give you this downloadable link of a message God gave me to preach at the PraiseDome. I hope you enjoy this message as I enjoyed bringing it forth. BE BLESSED!

Robert L. Bailey

For more information on me or my church, contact us @

Greater New Hope Church
10505 Bainbridge St.
Houston, TX 77016
www.greaternewhopechurch.org
www.restorationofpraise.org
pastor@restorationofpraise.org

About The Author

I am just a RADICAL MAN with a MIC and a MESSAGE about a MASTER who works MIRACLES. I believe that God has purposed me to be a SERVANT to SERVANTS, so I utilizes my gifts, talents, skills, and abilities to serve others as they serve God. I minister with the motto in mind that: I'M NOT SENT TO RECYCLE SAINTS, BUT I'M SENT TO RESTORE SOULS.

Labeled as "THE MIRACLE BABY", I am the 1st of 3 children born to Robert Bailey, Sr. and Shirley Bailey, who was told they couldn't have children. And since my youth, I've always been specially gifted to preach, sing, act, lead, and direct choirs. In 1999, I moved to Houston from Dallas and started establishing myself as a preacher and later a husband and father.

I am HAPPILY and WHOLEHEARTEDLY married to an amazing woman of 16 years (since Feb. 1, 2003), name Zahra` Rochelle Bailey and out of our union, the promise prophesied over us brought forth an amazing daughter, who was birthed on Feb. 28, 2017 name Zaila Rainn Bailey.

I've been afforded the opportunity to preach for over 40 years, since the age of 3 (licensed on Sept. 30, 1979, and ordained Feb. 2, 2003) and have been pastoring for 11 years, since Feb. 3, 2008. I founded a ministry named Restoration of Praise Fellowship, but in June of 2016, I was commissioned by God and asked by Dr. Claude E. Jenkins, Sr. to merge my ministry with the Greater New Hope Missionary Baptist Church. After a successful merger, I became the Senior Pastor and changed the name of the church to Greater New Hope Church, better known as The PraiseDome Nation. I am a very charismatic and energetic leader and preacher and have built a reputation around the world as an "unorthodox and inspiring" speaker, preacher, and singer.

I am a certified Christian counselor and have studied in various seminaries in Dallas, TX and in Houston, TX. I received my Masters and Bachelors of Divinity Degrees from Independent Bible College in Dallas, TX and received my Doctorate of Divinity Degree from St. Thomas Theological Seminary in Jacksonville, FL in April of 2018.

www.ingramcontent.com/pod-product-compliance
Lightning Source LLC
Chambersburg PA
CBHW050653160426
43194CB00010B/1925